GOOD

THINGS

COME

Good Things Come
Encountering God in Seasons Between Promises Given and Promises Fulfilled
ISBN: 978-1-944298-58-6

Cover and Interior Design by Luum Studio
Cover Photography by Lucas Silva Pinheiro Santos

LCCN: 2019914312

Printed in the United States of America
1 2 3 4 5 / 23 22 21 20 19

CAROLINE SCHANDEL

GOOD THINGS COME

ENCOUNTERING GOD IN SEASONS BETWEEN
PROMISES GIVEN AND PROMISES FULFILLED

TABLE OF CONTENTS

INTRODUCTION

For as long as I can remember I have loved to run. Not because I'm naturally good at it. My husband Mark is built like a runner and has won all kinds of awards and scholarships for it. But not me. I'm petite. My legs work extra hard to keep me moving long distances.

The reason I love running so much is because of how it makes me feel when I'm in that in-between space of *on the move* but *not yet there*. There's challenge woven into the journey, isn't there? Your body is pushed to further limits. Your mental strength actively works to keep you motivated. And your breathing must remain consistent, not too deep but also not too shallow.

A year ago we lived in this cute bungalow here in Atlanta and every few days I'd head out on another run. Each time I walked down my front steps and onto the sidewalk, I had a choice to make of which hill I was going to tackle that day. No matter what direction I picked, I had to begin my run by going uphill. I tried all of my options at one point or another. The steeper ones, which caused me to lose my breath within about a tenth of a mile, seemed exceptionally unkind for the beginning of a run. I finally settled on the route that started with a hill twice as long but not as harsh.

There's a personal conviction I live by in life, specifically that I don't walk up hills when I go running. I made the decision one day while in the middle of a run, when I instinctively started walking as I ascended the next hill. All of a sudden I became aware of what I was doing and it didn't make sense to me. Why would I train myself to decelerate when facing resistance? If I was doing this when running, then I was probably doing the same thing when facing other hard tasks. I didn't like the idea that I was easing up when things got difficult. So that day I quit walking up hills.

Now that I've moved to a new neighborhood in Atlanta, I don't run my usual route as often. But when I do, I know I'll be heading uphill within seconds of my feet hitting the pavement—and always with the conviction that I won't be walking this time. To ensure I follow through on my commitment, there are two things I do to make it all the way to the top.

At first, I keep my head down because I need to focus on one step after another. I'll never get there if I don't move my feet here. I watch them do their back and forth rhythm, willing them to not stop before I reach where I'm going.

But after a while I have to raise my head again, see how far I've made it, and remind myself of the vision. I'm not aimlessly ascending an eternal path of blacktop. There's a destination and direction to all of this. This isn't purposeless; this is intentional. I look around at where I am and set my sights once again on the end goal. Then, with my feet still moving, I watch as that final point gets a little closer.

Of course we rarely arrive as quickly as we want or thought we would, so after a while of looking ahead I can start feeling disheartened by how distant the hilltop still appears. Focusing ahead is motivating for a while, but then it abruptly switches to discouraging. In which case, I only have one option. Down my head goes again, staring at those faithful feet of mine and reminding myself that the only way I'll get there is by putting one foot in front of the other.

The whole back and forth is a dance of gazing up and looking down, lifting my eyes to the greater vision and fixing my sights on what's before me in the moment. It's a necessary practice because no matter how quickly I want to conquer that hill, the process always takes longer than I desire. Every single time.

Don't we all navigate the in-between of what hasn't happened or what we haven't seen or where we haven't arrived much longer—and more frequently—than we ever planned or imagined?

Maybe you're there right now, longing for a spouse while watching another friend get married, or for a baby you've prayed for years to hold, or for friends who would deeply know and love you. Maybe it's for the physical healing of a persistent sickness in your body or for your dream to manifest into an opportunity. Maybe it's for the mending of a broken heart, a letter of acceptance to the school of your dreams, the financial means to buy your first home, or the restoration of a broken relationship.

No matter the season you are in, life is never void of waiting. We all wander over a terrain full of questions and mysteries, obstacles and resistance. In each of our lives there are those places marked by the war of hoping in the middle of a reality that screams *not yet*. And despite the victories that do come our way, the levels of success we rise to or the influence we are entrusted with, we still wait. We never fully arrive. We remain standing amid the tension of hoping for what we sense somehow belongs to us though we haven't yet experienced it.

Even if we finally receive whatever it is we have longed for, we still wait. It's easy to dream only of our future destination, presuming that if we can just reach there then we will be happy and settled. This false promise boasts that at some point we will find ourselves where we no longer wait. But reality discloses a different message. The waiting never ceases because it is woven into the very thread of how we live. God moves in the waiting, is encountered in the waiting, and so reveals himself not in our arrival but in the tense middle as we wait.

The problem is that we are inundated with a message suggesting we fix and work, strive and push ourselves right out of our seasons of pause or delay. Especially if there's pain or discomfort to them, we're encouraged to do everything we can to avoid or bypass the journey.

But that's not what we read in the Bible. Repeatedly in the book of Psalms the call is simply to wait. By strength, stillness, and patience. For God's help, inheritance, and movement. Why? Because the waiting doesn't diminish or crush us. The waiting transforms and matures us.

As Paul wrote in Romans 8, "We are enlarged in the waiting. We, of course, don't see what is enlarging us. But the longer we wait, the larger we become, and the more joyful our expectancy." (vv. 35 The Message)

Waiting isn't about withholding. Waiting is about elevating, upgrading, and increasing. And God isn't on the outskirts of it, watching from a distance as we struggle our way through the process. He's right there in the middle of the tension with us, changing and championing us every step of the journey.

So if we aren't meant to eject or fix our way out of the mystery ingrained in today, then how do we navigate the seasons when we have no control over when, if, or how fulfillment manifests? How do we walk through another year of not knowing? How do we continue believing for the best as we carry the weight of disappointment for what still hasn't happened? How do we keep trusting God when he keeps us waiting?

The goal of this book is to invite you to find God in the mundane and often arduous rhythms of life where waiting does not reach its end and the fog of mystery lingers. Because learning to live in the middle of your present day transforms you. The uncertainties, questions, and tensions that comprise your season richen its very soil to be fertile with life-changing encounters.

These pages will activate and empower you to show up in the middle of exactly what is today with expectancy, gratitude, and the power to influence what is around you. This book isn't about passively waiting around until things change. It's about affecting what's before you as you anticipate God to do what only he can through you.

Together we will learn to live, breathe, and become in the waiting. Not because it's easy or simple, but because what is not yet is the place of greater faith. Imperfections, frustrations and loose ends are all components of our present reality. Here is where we are to live. And the uncertainty of it all is meant to draw us not to the God of answers but to the one of presence, who remains with us no matter what is before us.

The life we are called to live does not begin tomorrow. The place for us is here—today—thriving in the discomfort and mystery of what remains paused or delayed. Instead of trying to circumnavigate the tension, what if we trade our hopes of arrival for the journey of encounter?

For in the middle of our waiting, we experience God with us. Emmanuel. And where he is, is where we are meant to reside. It's where we become exactly who he's created us to be.

CHAPTER ONE

HIDDEN IN THE CLEFT

There I was standing before the "Big Swing." My best friend
Andi was strapped next to me and we were seconds away from
blindly being pushed off the edge of a wooden platform for what
was supposed to be the thrill of our lives.

I was terrified. My heart beat rapidly out of my chest and my
knees threatened to buckle at any moment. Yet I resolved not to
miss out on the experience, so I prayed and prophesied with extra
zeal as the impending drop crept closer.

With each pull of the harness around our legs and waist, the
reality became clear—the only way out was to be pushed off the platform, plain and simple.

I asked to have my straps checked one more time for good measure and when we were verified safe, Andi and I inched backwards
until our heels hung just over the edge. I closed my eyes, took a
deep breath, and thought about my body teetering 223 feet above
the earth of South Africa.

The man beside me grabbed the central harness that connected
Andi and I together by our waists and began counting loudly. He
held a wide grin on his face with each number he yelled.

Three...Two...One...

Push.

It's odd to reflect on moments like this. How something so fast—like falling 223 feet at 111 miles per hour in less than 3 seconds—can feel so eternal. Everything seems to go strangely silent. Like all of nature pauses to hold its own breath in wonder at this uninvited object plummeting through what was once a perfectly peaceful haven.

The silence that comes in this kind of waiting is thick and heavy. Loaded with tension and questions and bated breath. Your muscles are tightened, your mind goes blank, your heart may even slow its rhythm for a few seconds. You may think you know what will come, but still you are forced to wait. You are held captive by the present moment and surrendered to a process bigger than yourself. You carry no ability to determine or control what happens next.

❧

Andi and I plunged into the quiet abyss and waited for the falling to stop. We held our breath for the cord to stretch to its furthest point and tug us back up, confirming that our descent was complete.

Waiting is full of that kind of silence. The stillness that screams, "If something doesn't change and if the waiting doesn't break, this may crush me."

In all kinds of seasons I have found myself facedown on the floor, begging God to move me out of my waiting. Sometimes I can envision exactly where I want him to take me. Other times I am unsure as to how we (God and me) are going to get out of the stale, blank lobby of *not yet*. Either way, it's a crushing feeling. Breath short, tears plenty, and unsteady faith asking questions of where is he, how could he, and will he ever.

In my waiting I've witnessed how easy it is for me to turn my questions *on* God. I doubt if he cares or if I can trust him when he can't do this one thing for me. I wonder if he will remember me, look upon me, or move on my behalf again. It's tempting to determine him to be the cause, catalyst, and agent for all I'm enduring.

But there are other questions for us to ask. Because the waiting is meant to transform us.

If we tune in, we can shift our questions toward discovering the value of waiting. We can ask ourselves what we will choose to do in the midst of those not yets—how we will respond, who we will become, and what we are meant to catch, take hold of, and put on.

Life won't always be the way it is now. Our circumstances will likely and eventually shift in some direction. So in seasons of waiting we are invited into transformation by allowing ourselves to engage in the middle of what is. Instead of asking when our conditions will improve or why God doesn't seem to be with us, we can embrace the waiting and let it change us from within.

Waiting isn't designed to freeze us from moving, dreaming, or doing. Instead, it is an opportunity for us to partner with its transforming nature. Waiting leads us to walk as people of expectation, purpose, and confidence who know and trust that God will move when we cannot see...yet. There we must decide who we will be when no one watches and what we will dream for when we cannot taste it. The ground of waiting won't depart from us. But if we inhabit it, if we put our feet on it and allow it to work through us, we will walk away transformed.

⚜

Tucked into the early part of the book of Luke is the story of Jesus' temptation in which "he was led by the Spirit in the wilderness for forty days, being tempted by the devil" (Luke 4:1-2). This sounds like a pretty intense situation, especially at the onset of his ministry. But what's so important to recognize here is that Jesus was brought into the wilderness by God himself.

This wasn't a passive season in which Jesus coasted through the desert grounds. It wasn't forty days void of opposition, hunger, or temptation. Rather, it was a season of fasting and praying out of obedience to his Father in order to prepare for what would be done in the places and with the people ahead.

This ground also wasn't without tension. Jesus was surrounded by nothing living, the sun was scorching, and all was arid. Three times within this desert season Satan tempted him to turn from God. Three times Jesus refused to give in by speaking truth. After forty days "the devil had ended every temptation" (vv. 13) and left Jesus, who by this time was very hungry (vv. 2).

Yet despite all that happened in the desert, what is striking about this account is that out of this season, "Jesus returned in the power of the Spirit to Galilee" (vv. 14). Jesus transitioned out of the wilderness to begin his public ministry now full of the transforming power of God. Luke begins this chapter saying that Jesus was already "full of the Holy Spirit" (vv. 1) from being baptized at the Jordan River, at which time the Holy Spirit came upon him like a dove. But now, after his temptation and forty days in the desert, he returns full of the *power* of the Spirit.

Out of the desert season came an empowerment. The barren environment did not hinder God from filling and fueling his Son for where he was sending him next.

When we're waiting on those big promises and feel as though the delay may crush us, or when we can't control the outcome even if we try, or when we feel powerless against our circumstances, the most important resource available to us the Holy Spirit. In the midst of uncertainty we can pray, believe, and ask that through this season we will be filled with the power of God.

What if the ground of waiting is the same ground where we are empowered by the Spirit? What if the waiting of today could prepare and commission us to such an extent that we are able to transform the atmosphere around us?

Think about something you're waiting on. Most likely your attention and thoughts orbit around how you can work your way out of the waiting. But instead of burning time and attention on exit strategies, what if you released control and let the process transform you?

That's the kind of waiting I'm talking about. Not the waiting that gets us what we want, but the waiting that changes us. The waiting that fills us to overflowing and sends us out to influence the environment, people, and relationships around us. The waiting that allows God's Spirit to first move in and through us so we can impact the world from a place of sincere transformation.

A few years after my swing experience in South Africa, which we thankfully lived to tell about, Mark and I spent a summer in Pemba, Mozambique. We were students of the Harvest School with Iris Ministries, a school designed to equip and commission missionaries to the farthest reaches of the world. We weren't certain it was the direction God was leading us long-term, but we desired a season to learn from powerful leaders and receive vision from God for our future. So we packed up our newlywed life in Georgia and headed off on a summer adventure.

One particular morning in Pemba we heard from Sean Feucht, founder of the Burn24/7 movement. Sean didn't talk to our group for long, but I locked in as he began describing the function of a slingshot. If you've ever shot one, then you know how it works. You pull the rubber band back as far as it can go and then you release it, propelling your ammunition with impressive force. It's counterintuitive that you would pull it *back* to send it *forward*, but that's the way to create momentum. The farther you draw it back, the farther you launch it forward.

The waiting ground is precisely that moment between the generation and release of momentum, when the rubber band is taut and thin with no slack remaining. If you listen closely, you'll notice that when the slingshot is loaded with tension it carries noise. The waiting heralds the message that whatever is about to shoot forth is going to launch far.

How ironic to consider that our waiting seasons carry the purpose of sending. That something so still, silent, and strained could be the means for projecting us far ahead.

It makes no sense. Yet time and again the waiting of life confirms that only by being pulled back are we propelled distances far beyond our reach.

Waiting precedes action. The launching pad of forward progression is a place of pause, rest, and stillness.

❧

Exodus 33 reveals how God leverages the waiting to launch his people into their destinies. There at Mount Horeb it was finally time for God's people to get up and get going. He had commissioned Moses to leave their current place and Moses pushed back saying that he had to know that God would go with him. This was the cry of a man unwilling to move ahead of God's own presence, to which God promised, "My Presence will go with you, and I will give you rest" (vv. 14). In the midst of being commissioned, Moses and his people were promised rest. Not victory, wealth, or promotion but rest in the presence of God.

Moses then boldly demanded that God not only go with him but also show him his glory. God promised that "I will make all my goodness pass before you and will proclaim before you my name 'The Lord.'...But...you cannot see my face, for man shall not see me and live." (vv. 19-20)

God agreed to Moses' request. He would go with him. But in order for that to happen, Moses had to hide away in the waiting. Moses wasn't being banished into obscurity for nothing. God was placing him there because he intended to go before and with him on the journey ahead. While Moses was in the waiting, the glory and goodness of God would pass before him. But Moses could not behold it. God tucked Moses into the cleft of a rock and covered him by his hand until he had passed by in front of him (vv. 21-23).

Moses, clear in his calling to lead the people, was made to step into hiddenness.

I wonder how many of us know the feeling of being put aside. Maybe you've been commissioned. Maybe you are even able to see the place God is calling you to go. Yet for some reason you are standing in the wilderness, waiting in the cleft of a rock.

You may feel you've been tucked away into a place of total obscurity and wonder if God has forgotten his plans for you. You may be in a place of opposition, temptation, or struggle, asking why God would ever send you here. You may question if you've been overlooked or abandoned.

So many voices today tell us to find the quickest way to push eject, to muster up strength and move ourselves out of the waiting. They boast efficiency, elevation, and promotion, suggesting that waiting isn't part of the process so get moving.

But the truth is, the God who brought you into this season will bring you through it. He hasn't placed you into the waiting for nothing. It isn't void of power or plans. In fact, he may be passing by in goodness and glory to carry his purpose ahead of you. And it may be your willingness to step aside and agree with the season of waiting for his advance that will allow his goodness to move before you.

The waiting ground is loaded with uncertainty. But if you can choose to stay in it, not ejecting yourself too quickly or desperately looking for a shortcut, there is the promise of transformation by the power of the Spirit.

God does not abandon his people. He calls, leads, sends, and commissions them, but he does not forsake them. He does not forget them. He does not give up on them.

Wherever you find yourself in the waiting, rest. You are in the middle of the power of the Spirit coming upon you. You are being pulled into the pause that comes prior to being sent into the land God has promised you. Like a slingshot, the tense strain of today that makes you want to scream and shout and get yourself moving may be the best indication that God is preparing to send you.

༞

Back in high school I dealt with all kinds of insecurities. I rarely felt like I fit in even though I was surrounded by caring friends and involved in a plethora of activities. I struggled with my looks, often wondering if I was pretty enough to be noticed or pursued. I questioned if I was good enough, analyzing every little detail and beating myself up for how I wasn't measuring up to my unattainable standards.

But there was one insecurity of mine that dominated the others and that was my struggle to use my voice. I often felt too self-conscious to speak up. I'd second guess anything I was about to say, choosing to be quiet over taking the risk I'd say something wrong or stupid. Even with all my friends and activities, I held back throughout most of high school. I never could get over how uncomfortable I felt with voicing my opinions.

One of my worst high school memories was as a junior at the awards ceremony for my field hockey team. It was the end of the season and everyone was given a paper plate award. They mostly referenced funny inside jokes from the season. Mine was "most likely to be silent" with a whole bunch of "shhhhhs" drawn on it. I was so embarrassed. It felt like one giant confirmation that I obviously didn't have anything important to say.

My struggle with my voice carried into college. When I transferred schools right before my sophomore year, I was warmly welcomed into a community of lively, brilliant women. Yet still I sensed that there was this muzzle on my mouth that prevented me from speaking out the words that were really in me. I felt trapped but also clueless about how to overcome it.

Right before my senior year I spent a summer in Kenya with a group of other college students. One afternoon while in a local village, our group leaders asked for a volunteer to share with the community about our faith in Jesus. Without giving it a thought, I shot up my hand. In that moment my fear collided with my courage, and I was picked to preach my very first sermon...ever.

I stepped onto a rickety, wooden platform in this remote village with a crowd gathering all around me. My hair was in two braided pigtails and I was dressed up in my best maxi skirt. One hand held a microphone and the other had my Bible. With eyes set on the faces in the crowd, I shared about the goodness of God to overcome even our greatest weaknesses by his power. It wasn't long or noteworthy, but I *knew* as I stepped down from the platform that preaching was exactly what I was made to do for the rest of my life.

You'd think after such a defining moment of awakening that I would come back to college fully confident in my voice. Yet I still battled the same fears and insecurities. I felt just as closed up. I longed for God's instant breakthrough to free my voice and lift whatever muzzle felt like it was on me but despite all my prayers and pleas, nothing happened.

By the time I graduated I had done enough inner soul work through counseling and prayer to identify key memories and fears that caused me the most trapping with my voice. I had ditched the lies I could easily recognize. I even felt like I was coming into some confidence with my voice. But still there was no major breakthrough.

After spending the next year interning for a youth ministry in Colorado, I packed up my belongings and left for a year of travel, service, and self-discovery. This was when everything changed for me and it all took place one evening in India.

At the time our large group of twenty-five young adults was spending a couple days debriefing together before entering an-other month of ministry. We were tired, overwhelmed, and in need of some serious rest. Thankfully our organization set us up for two nights at a local hotel where air-conditioning was plentiful and the beds were heavenly.

On our second night we gathered to worship together. There was a general heaviness to the atmosphere. Some teammates were ques-tioning if it was time to head home. Others were mad at their friend next to them. A lot were exhausted by the pace of the whole year.

But God was doing something different in me that night. I wasn't weighed down. Instead, I could feel his fire. It felt like God's word was burning in me, similar to what Jeremiah described when he wrote, "his word is in my heart like a fire, a fire shut up in my bones. I am weary of holding it in; indeed, I cannot." (Jeremiah 20:9) All those years of praying, believing, stepping out of my comfort zone, and waiting for God's breakthrough culminated here. God's word burned in me to the point that I no longer could hold it in.

During an instrumental lull in the worship set I stood up and I spoke. No one asked me to, but I knew I had to. What flowed from my mouth were words of faith, boldness, and confidence. They spoke to our identity and calling in God's kingdom. They were everything I had been scared to speak for too long and finally they flowed. As each word shot from my lips, it felt like that muzzle was loosening and falling off right in front of me. Because this wasn't about pleasing or performing for anyone but about stepping into who God made me to be in a moment that demanded it.

Everything changed for me that night. My breakthrough came and God launched me out after years of waiting, hoping, and asking for him to set me free.

※

Looking back now I can pinpoint how gracious God was in not instantly freeing me of my pain and fear with my voice. It didn't feel like it at the time, of course. But had he done so, it would have removed me from my own process of growing along the journey. I needed to wrestle, fight, and be changed as I waited for my breakthrough. It's how I found my voice. Not through instantaneous freedom but the quiet, hidden work of God walking with me through facing lies and standing upon fears.

The testimony of God awakening my voice is one I will never quit sharing because of how he moved and released me. But the process was not quick or easy. It was purposeful and hidden. I waited years for God to liberate my voice. All those tears in high school. All those prayers in college. Even after uncovering how he wants to use my voice, still things weren't immediately different. It was a journey of wrestling in the quiet place.

There in the waiting I encountered him. There my voice was awakened. There I became. And when the moment arrived, he shot me out full of fire, passion, and a testimony that if God can do this in my life, he certainly can do this for you.

⋇

There's so much to be said on waiting as we journey ahead, so much about God's purpose and power in the middle of what is still not yet.

What I've come to recognize is that even as I have experienced breakthrough in a certain area, there are always others that remain unanswered. From such repetition I have wrapped my head around the fact that waiting isn't a stop we pass through on our journey with God. Waiting is woven into our story, season after season. It is the ground of faith, the place we encounter the God who is with us right where we are.

Whatever the waiting is for you, he is in it with you. Not distant, indifferent, or distracted. He is Emmanuel. God with us, who has purposed that no matter the season we walk in he will use it to transform us. For as he is the God who moves us *from* glory to glory

(2 Corinthians 3:18), so also he is the God who moves *with* us.

The waiting of life invites God to meet us right where we are. The working of the Spirit is found when all seems barren, forgotten, and without. There, when life is paused, silent, and hidden, God's Spirit moves. His goodness passes before us in order to be with us where we are sent ahead.

CHAPTER TWO

STANDING STILL

For years I was in a place of perpetual waiting, hoping for God to fulfill the desire I longed for more than any other—to be a wife, live beside my husband, and embark on a wild journey together.

Due to his seemingly eternal absence, I launched around the world on my own. I jumped into a fast-paced ministry of adventure that led me to over forty countries in five years. I resolved to live a full life and deeply hoped that along the way, somewhere, I would find him beside me in the same orbit.

Some days it was easy to remind myself that the wait was worth it and God was in it. Others were filled with doubts over if my dream would ever realize given how long it had been with no sign. Those days the tears fell hard. Waiting for something you want so badly and having no control over how or when to make it happen can be excruciatingly difficult. I'm guessing you know the feeling.

In the middle of one of those seasons when my heart ached beyond comprehension for someone I didn't even know, I scribbled a specific verse with a dry erase marker on the mirror of my apartment bathroom. Every morning and night I would look at it, speak it out loud, and do all I could to settle into its truth in the midst of my spinning

"I am still confident of this: I will see the goodness of the Lord in the land of the living. Wait for the Lord. Be strong and take heart, and wait for the Lord." (Psalm 27:13-14 NIV)

If this was what God promised, I reasoned, then this was the truth I would cling to no matter what I felt or how little I saw. I kept believing that despite the prolonged waiting ground I stood upon, richly watered by my tears, I would see God's goodness. I would partake of it, taste it, and know it.

Of every word in the verse on my bathroom mirror, the one I held closest was *still*. I am still confident of this. Still implies waiting. It suggests that time is passing without the fulfillment of a promise. It means that the one who waits must keep their confidence in the face of doubt and delay.

Despite all that has not happened, I will *still* see it—God's promise alive and active in my life.

Ten years after first asking God to fulfill my desire for my husband, that man showed up. Of course it looked nothing like I imagined it would. It wasn't sparkly or pretty or glamorous; it was living and breathing and messy. Sure signs God's hands were in all of it.

On a chilly March morning on the shores of St. Simons Island, God fulfilled my long-awaited hope. There I stood in front of Mark. Bent on one knee. With a ring. Asking me to be his wife.

After the ring was slipped on my finger and I said "yes" over and over again, Mark stood to his feet and I embraced him. Tucked in close to him, I looked over his shoulder at the endless ocean in the distance. The water seemed to fall off the world's edge. The moment was frozen. All was still, silent, and paused.

As I absorbed the sheer vastness of it all, I replayed in my mind the last decade of waiting—the moments of being sure I had found him, the nights curled up on my bedroom floor weeping over a hope still unmet, the years of watching others find what I longed for myself. Every memory carried the whisper of the same voice, repeating words of promise year after year and season after season.

Beloved, I am good.

Standing on that beach, embracing my soon-to-be husband, I wept. For the better part of an hour I repeatedly uttered the words, "God, you are so good. You are *so* good."

❧

Though it can feel this way at times, the waiting ground isn't the land where all hopes go to die. The absence of whatever you're waiting for today does not negate the presence of it ahead.

Instead, the waiting ground is the birthing place for promises. Only by waiting in the still of today are we able to partake in all God's goodness declared for us in the land of the living. Even so, those desires are tricky to navigate, difficult to hope for, and painful to wait upon.

Most of us hold closely to what we believe are promises from God. Whether they came to us as a divine encounter, a whisper in the chaos, or from the pages of a worn Bible, we carry them as a part of us.

Some days we can become bitter to them, as though they are reminders of everything we don't have. We consider the words or recall the moments as though they tell us what will not be and how we should forget them. We throw them across the room, ensuring they hit the wall with force before falling to the ground. We decide to deprive them of attention in hopes they feel the pain we ourselves feel by the reminder of what is not. But then a few moments, days, or months later we return to that spot and pick them up. We brush them off and decide to hope again for what we cannot see. Our method of neglecting, rejecting, and ignoring didn't bring much life so we decide to try a friendlier way.

Certain days we choose to take matters into our hands, grasping for total control of the situation and refusing to take no for an answer. We focus our prayers and discussion on how to ensure that our hopes will manifest as quickly as possible. We give little thought to our transformation in the middle of the process and full attention to the promise's realization. Without intending to, we can displace God's leading from the entire journey by our desperate need for arrival.

Or on other days we disqualify ourselves from the possibility of the promise occurring altogether. We examine the reasons that such a dream would never be possible for us given our past history, messy present, or lack of qualifications. We justify our stance by the facts, current reality, or words others have spoken over us. We determine to abandon whatever silly promise we sensed God was stirring within us, chalking it up to foolishness versus the possibility that maybe God is wanting to upgrade us beyond where we have been.

Without a doubt it is difficult to steward something with grace and confidence when we have no control over when, if, or how it will happen. Even if we can find a way to carry faith for the if or take guesses on the how, the when, that uncertain *when*, remains elusive.

❧

A few years ago I woke up one Tuesday morning to plan my Bible Study for that evening. Fifteen women were showing up at my apartment and the week prior had been so busy I hadn't prepared anything until a few hours before they were scheduled to arrive. Given how much time the other teachings had taken me, I wasn't sure I'd be able to generate a substantial lesson.

I cracked open my Bible. We were reading through the book of Mark, so each week was mostly predetermined. I flipped to the next segment in our study and began reading a chapter in which Jesus was discussing the end times.

"What the heck am I going to say about all of this?" I asked myself, fully aware of how little time I had to prepare.

Knowing my panic wouldn't get me far, I let myself sink into the words on the page. Fairly quickly something hit me as I read through chapter 13.

Leaving the temple, one of Jesus' disciples pointed out the massive stones and buildings around them. He made note of the greatness he physically saw. Jesus responded to all who could hear saying that what was before them would not stand. "Do you see these great buildings? There will not be left here one stone upon another that will not be thrown down." (Mark 13:2) That's a surprising thing to hear and it puzzled his listeners. Jesus told them what was to come and his friends instantly wanted to know more.

Capitalizing on a quiet moment when Jesus was sitting on the Mount of Olives, Peter, James, John, and Andrew approached him. I have no doubt they were hoping Jesus would reveal more to them since he was away from the crowd. They jumped right in to ask him what they were reeling about ever since Jesus mentioned it. "Tell us, when will these things happen? And what will be the sign that they are all about to be fulfilled?" (vv. 4 NIV)

Both questions essentially targeted the same thing. The answer his disciples were searching for was *when*. They wanted to know which signs to look for so they could know when the fulfillment of his prophecy was getting close.

Jesus then assured them that it would happen, but he didn't give them a timeline. His response didn't assuage their deep desire to know more specifically…when.

Each time I read this account I see myself in it. I am intimately acquainted with the desire to know details. The promise of *what* only fuels my desire to know *when* it's going to happen. Countless times I find myself quietly sitting with God, hearing him whisper to me. The promises are beautiful, terrifying, or somewhere in between. My response is always to wonder when it will come to pass. *I hear you, God. Tell me when. Tell me the signs. Tell me how. But mostly, tell me when.*

The same thing happens with my three-year-old, Eloise. When I tell her we're going to take a trip to see her Nana and Popi, some of her very favorite people in this world, all she wants to know is when. Is it today? Tomorrow? Next week?

The knowledge of something yet to come naturally stirs a desire to know more. It's difficult to let the what linger in our lives without pressing for more information. We want our promises to be clear. We don't mind waiting if we know how long it will last. It's the uncertainty that makes the waiting ground so fertile with doubt and frustration.

The amazing thing about this exchange in Mark 13 is that even when Jesus was with his friends in a quiet place away from the crowd and even when he was asked the most direct questions, he still remained silent on when. He described in great detail what would come, explaining what the signs would be. Then he was explicit: "But concerning that day or that hour, no one knows, not even the angels in heaven, nor the Son, but only the Father" (vv. 32).

His friends were standing right there with Jesus, in flesh and blood. They had no reason to doubt whether they were hearing clearly what he was saying. The words all came directly from his mouth. Still, they could not learn when.

How wild is it to realize that even Jesus didn't know. He too must wait in the uncertainty of when this promise would come to pass.

Oftentimes God withholds answers to our questions, especially those demanding timestamps, to keep our faith and his mystery alive. Even sitting on the mountain with his closest friends, Jesus preserved the mystery. He didn't extend answers. He held space for them to lean in and believe even when they did not fully know or understand.

Why? So their faith would remain active in the waiting. A guarantee on exactly when things would happen would have hindered them from a vibrant faith. If we have all the answers then faith is not necessary. Only in the unknown were the disciples forced to rely on an active relationship with God. Only in the mystery were they led to trust, hope, and believe. Only by waiting in faith would more people be drawn to follow after them.

It's not by maintaining control that we are compelled to live with hope; it's by living and breathing faithfully through the process as we still anticipate what's ahead.

We can be certain that the promises of God will always require faith. And that unknown when upgrades our trust, hope, and perseverance. No matter how much we try, we cannot escape the mystery woven throughout the promises we hold. No matter the power of our prayers, maturity of our words, or depth of our character, the mystery remains.

At times this can be a comfort. Our lives are being held in hands so much greater than our own. Yet other times it's difficult to navigate. We believe if we could just see how long the road is going to be, the process might become easier, smoother, and more graceful.

The battle of doubt and frustration we face in the not yet isn't about the promises themselves but the mystery attached to them. Mystery is uncomfortable and stretching. It keeps us dependent. It withholds answers and prevents us from taking control. But it also compels us to be transparent, raw, and open as we wait one more day, and then another, wavering between weariness and hope. It presses us to recognize what's before us and willingly participate in the story at hand.

So the questions we wrestle with lead us through a process designed to change us at the core. Whether we love or hate it at any given moment, God prioritizes the journey over the destination. He cares far more about who we become and how we progress rather than where or when we arrive.

We can't shortcut the process in order to arrive prematurely, because we won't get there until we catch hold of the faith, grit, and character we are meant to develop along the way.

The mystery of the promise is never something to conquer. It's to be received as a gracious invitation to activate a faith that surpasses circumstance. The choice to hope for what we cannot see and believe for more than what we can feel is ultimately faith extended beyond ourselves. It is faith in tune with the God who is much greater than one we can hold in our hands.

⚘

One of the passages in the Bible that always fuels me is found in the beginning of the book of Joshua. Moses had died and God told Joshua it was now his turn to lead the Israelites into the Promised Land, where God had vowed to his people for centuries they would dwell.

What I love about this story and Joshua specifically is that he was developed in the desert. Through all the wanderings, grumblings, and encounters in that barren land, Joshua was built into the leader who was ready to shepherd Israel after Moses' death. He found his calling. Joshua cultivated the strength and character necessary for what came next. Long before he saw it himself, God was moving ahead of him.

Now it was time for Joshua to lead the Israelites into the land yet the size and strength of its inhabitants terrified God's people. Those who scouted it out had come back feeling like grasshoppers in the presence of giants. Even though God was calling them there, the people felt no confidence it could be theirs given what they had seen.

Joshua was commissioned as leader for this whole company of people. He was to go into a foreign place, conquer giants, and take over a land he knew nothing about. Yet, even though he had no idea how it would take place, he went because God promised it to him. And that was enough for him. The promise of God was all he needed to walk into the impending challenges.

This is what most promises are like. When God begins speaking about where he wants to take us, so often it calls for a confidence beyond anything we have in the present moment. We may feel unqualified or unequipped. Yet God's intention is always that what is to come will require us to increase our faith and courage.

God does not leave us alone in the process. He promised Joshua that he would go with him: "I will be with you. I will not leave you or forsake you" (Joshua 1:5). Though so much of the journey is unknown, God commits his presence to us.

God charged Joshua to go by his promise to a land he did not know and lead an entire people to their destiny: "Be strong and courageous, for you shall cause this people to inherit the land that I swore to their fathers to give them. Only be strong and very courageous." (vv. 6-7) This exchange reveals that strength and courage are the companions needed to navigate the process between promise and fulfillment. Strength and courage, always. Because strength keeps us standing and courage keeps us moving forward. So when we are pressing into and believing for the promises of God, how necessary they are on the journey. They keep us upright and advancing even when all may feel wildly intimidating or painfully unclear.

Joshua carried a promise in the midst of uncertainty. He knew so little and still he went. Still he trusted. Still he embraced the process and his calling to see the promise of God fulfilled before his eyes. Even as he waited in the mysteries of the moment, he listened, followed, and obeyed.

God extends the same invitation your way—to walk in trust beyond sight and encounter the God of presence instead of clamoring for the God of answers.

For there life births from your waiting. Upon that ground God creates. He gives breath and dimension to long-awaited promises. Though you may not see or feel it, God is moving. He is at work deeper than your feelings and the affirmations of others, which is something you cannot afford to forget.

So this is the holy charge of waiting. You are tasked to believe, hope, and stand firm for what you cannot yet see.

Though it challenges you, the tension of this is the gift. Because it transitions you from passively waiting to intimately engaging with God. When you grasp the tense nature of waiting, you understand what David meant in Psalm 27. Right after saying he was confident of the goodness he would see, he proclaimed with conviction: "Wait for the Lord; be strong, and let your heart take courage; wait for the Lord!" (vv. 14)

These words are infused with military language. David knew what it was like to live with adversaries and foes encamped around him. When surrounded by enemies, he stood firm against whatever might appear. No matter what is around me, he said, "though war arise against me, yet I will be confident" (vv. 3). David carried the courage that he would see God's goodness. And his conviction for beholding the promise was simply to wait.

Wait by strength. Wait by taking heart and having courage. Wait active and alive, alert to the lies that spring up from this ground and remain aware of God's presence.

These words mirror what God spoke to Joshua as he charged him to go into a land he didn't know. Be active and fiercely take up courage as you wait.

Waiting isn't about sitting on the sidelines. Waiting is about tapping into an inner strength. There is nothing easy about the waiting process. It's about being alive and alert in the middle of the mystery no matter the opposition, uncertainties, or delays.

Even as I waited for the day I would begin life alongside my husband, the unknowns remained. I often read the words on my bathroom mirror and would decide in my heart once again that despite all I couldn't see, I would trust and hope for what God was doing. Those words never carried guarantees as to how, when, or if things would turn out a certain way. The act of waiting drew me into hoping with God. To settle in my faith that no matter what I saw or how I felt, God's goodness was present. His goodness was ahead. And he was right there with me in the mystery.

❧

I often find myself attempting to separate the waiting from the promise, expecting that after a season of pause I will shake the dust off my feet, gratefully finished with the postponement, and take those celebratory steps into fulfillment. It's easy for me to approach my waiting ground as the land where I stand now but that one day I will move into the place of promise. Yet in doing so, I miss a key element to it all.

What if instead the land you are standing on today *is* the land from which promises will spring up? What if rather than a holding cell, you see your season as fertile ground for partnership with God to bring forth life and promise?

To see the waiting as a part of the promise is to move yourself from being a participant in a rigged game of fate to actively partnering in what unfolds. When you embrace this great "both/and"—the waiting and the promise—you catch vision for the responsibility you have in the process. You become a steward of purpose, not a passive pawn allowing what may come to play out.

The waiting ground is where promises erupt and vibrant life arises from mere dirt.

So let the mystery ingrained in the process afford you the opportunity to grow in faith, hope, and confidence right where you are. Let the mystery of waiting dissolve your dependency upon circumstances, elevating it to its proper place where it is built by trusting in the process and resting in the unknown.

God transforms. That is who he is. He takes what is barren and formless, and he creates. Instead of offering us more promising circumstances or supplies that are easier to work with, he brings life from what seems impossible.

If your feet are planted upon a land of unfulfilled promises, if you are tensely waiting as the wind of doubt whips around you, then stand with courage.

Wait. Watch. God is moving.

CHAPTER THREE

THE STORM

On my second trip around the world, I led a group of forty young adults on their journey to eleven different countries. I had recently completed my own yearlong adventure and it showed. Fresh-faced travelers arrived with shiny new backpacks and never-slept-in tents, while both of mine were covered in stains and dirt. Each mark carried a story with it, whether it was from the Malawian bush, Amazon jungle, or Thai countryside. There was no mistaking that my tent, pack, and the rest of my gear had been through some wild experiences.

When I found out that we would be camping by the Irish seaside for a few weeks, I expected a relatively luxe time with gorgeous weather and western amenities. Overlooking the crashing waves of the endless ocean and considering some of the places I had previously pitched camp, I thought we had it made.

What I didn't anticipate were the levels of rain and wind that would blow through. It was August in Ireland, a month in which the days are unusually sunny. Just after sunrise and all through the day, it was picture-perfect weather. The sun was shining brightly and the temperatures remained in the low seventies.

But those late afternoons and evenings told a different story. Within moments, unexpected rainstorms burst forth and the winds whipped in all directions.

Pretty quickly throughout our stay my tent revealed that it wasn't as young or agile as it once was. Thanks to all those afternoon storms, water started seeping through the bottom of my tent and waking me up morning after morning to cold, wet puddles. Being the resourceful leader I was (trying to be), I grabbed a couple trash bags out of the communal bathroom and covered my tent floor with them.

But then holes started appearing in my rainfly. They allowed for water to steadily drip onto the interior mesh lining of my tent, and right onto me. No problem, I thought. A covering of duct tape and my tent would be as good as new.

Then one night the hurricane came. Our tents were positioned along the wide, grassy edge of a cliff so there was no coverage to speak of, causing the wind to whip through our campsite without intervention. I awoke to my tent poles bowing in so hard that they were about ready to break. Rain was coming through my once-patched-up holes and water was seeping through the edges of my trash bag floor. My arms were extended as far as they could reach, alternating which two tent poles I was trying to keep from snapping in half. Not only that, but the corners of my tent were no longer staked to the ground. My casual hammering of a couple weeks ago wasn't ready for such a violent storm. So as the winds whipped through, all my tent corners pulled up.

It was a ridiculous scene of comedy and error. Promotional videos for this wild journey always recount highlights of community, ministry, and adventure. What could really add some color would be to record this wild scene—me as a petite woman, extending her not-so-long arms in all directions, doing all she could to keep her tent from dying a most sudden, tragic death.

If you ever need a good picture of what determination looks like, think of me at three in the morning with my headlamp askew, my five layers of clothes piled on to keep me warm and dry, water seeping up from the ground into my tent, rain driving down overhead, and those tent poles threatening to snap with one powerful gust. Amidst it all, I was resolved that this storm would not blow me over or destroy my tent. With ferocity and focus, I settled that those winds would not move me.

The storm eventually died down and by morning the group emerged one by one to survey the damage. Some came wandering out of the bathroom where they had chosen to hunker down for the night, a smart move I thought. Others casually unzipped their brand new, high quality tents without a clue as to what had happened the night before. My faithful tent and I survived, but it never made it out of that Irish campsite. It had done its duty, keeping me from being blown away and managing to withstand total collapse in the middle of the storm.

I think back to that night as such a clear example of how fear is like a wind that disorients and dislodges us as we traverse the ground between promise and fulfillment. Fear attempts to misalign us from our purpose and disengage us from our process.

Think about where you are right now. Where are you tensely waiting for breakthrough even though your current reality is quiet or stagnant? How is fear blowing in on you? What is it wanting to stir up? Where is it trying to move you?

No matter the circumstances surrounding your waiting, fear is always present doing what it can to pull you from the place God has planted you. To keep you from progressing, changing, and growing. To instill chaos within you so that you believe that the only way to find peace again is to move out of the season you're in.

With the waiting ground already vulnerable enough, fear tries to pervert the mystery of it into a confirmation that you are lost. Fear whispers that the waiting is pointless and that no life will come from here. It is all for nothing, it says, so give up, walk away, and forget it. So crafty is fear that it will try to turn your discouragement into perceived enlightenment that if you simply take matters into your own hands, things will improve. While wisdom can provoke you to actively step out and into new territory with God, fear will use shame and despair to frenziedly propel you forward.

Much like the whipping winds that tried to dislodge my entire tent (and me) from being grounded, fear seeks to disconnect and disengage you from your identity, promises, and the presence of God.

❧

The tension of faith and waiting is that we must believe and hope for what we do not see, even as the winds stir. This is why God repeatedly says that those who are in process, those who are waiting, those who have yet to receive and are "looking forward" (Hebrews 11:10), are not to fear no matter the storm or circumstance.

There's a powerful story in the New Testament that I often go back to no matter what season I am in. It's found in a few places, including Mark 4. Right before this passage Jesus taught parables to those listening by the water. By now it was getting dark and evening had come, so Jesus told his disciples they needed to move to the other side of the lake (vv. 35). They all hopped in a wooden boat on the Sea of Galilee. It wasn't too big or fancy, just a simple boat for the journey.

The disciples were out on the water with Jesus and a giant storm swelled up—the waves crashed, waters stirred, and winds swirled. Utter chaos ensued. Just as the water started overcoming the boat, fear began overwhelming the disciples.

But Jesus was in a completely different state, comically sleeping in the middle of the chaos. I love that not only was he asleep, but Mark points out that Jesus was on a cushion within this meek wooden boat. He wasn't just resting, he was comfortable doing it. But the disciples were unwilling to let him stay sleeping because of what was happening, so they awoke him saying, "Teacher, do you not care that we are perishing?" (vv. 38)

Isn't this something we often do? We think just because God isn't quickly, actively, or frantically moving on our behalf, that somehow he doesn't care for us. We equate God's instant rescue with confirmation that he loves us.

If that's true, then why wasn't Jesus moving? Why was he sleeping through the storm? Because he had already told them exactly where they were going. Even with the storm swirling and waves crashing, Jesus was resting because he wasn't concerned about the circumstances. He knew they were going to the other side. The disciples were consumed by their surroundings, not focused on what had been promised. What they saw with their eyes overrode what had been spoken to them. The seen overwhelmed the unseen and, in allowing this to happen, fear and chaos whipped them around with force and frenzy.

Instead of joining Jesus in his comfortable place of rest in the middle of the storm, they woke him. Jesus rose and rebuked the raging sea around them with the words, "Peace! Be still!" (vv. 39) With that simple command, the winds and waves died down and a calm came across the water. All was suddenly quiet.

Can you imagine the transition from a wild storm to serene water? Not only did the surroundings become hushed, but I'm guessing the disciples did too. As the Son of God spoke from a place of rest and peace, everything paused to witness the moment.

Then looking at his disciples he asked them, "Why are you so afraid? Have you still no faith?" (vv. 40)

The disciples were so caught up in what was happening around them and what could happen to them that they totally forgot who was with them and what he was doing in the middle of the storm. Jesus, the Son of God, lay sleeping in that boat because of what he knew—both who he was and where they were going.

Circumstances did not take hold of his rest, identity, or trust in the process. Instead, he knew that his authority to settle the storm came from his ability to sleep in the middle of it.

Yet the disciples lost sight of who was with them, what he promised, and where they were going. They missed the opportunity to rise above their panic and calm the environment around them. Fear wholly disoriented them from their process and purpose.

When our eyes are focused only on what we can see, we forget what has been promised. When we forget the promises we've been given, we can find ourselves thrown about in a frenzy rather than quieting the chaos by the rest within us.

Fear seeks to detach us from our identities and make us forget who we are. It wants to dislodge us from God's promises so we choose unbelief instead of trust in what God has spoken. Ultimately, fear tries to move us out of the waiting ground. It plants seeds of worry that say if we don't frantically, forcefully, and immediately take matters into our own hands, nothing will come from this place of waiting.

This is why God commands us not to fear more than any other command in the Bible. Fear seeks to steal our identity and redirect us on a path away from our destiny and calling.

Yet what's important to understand about fear is that it's always coupled with an invitation: the opportunity *to fear not.*

To fear not means that with courage and boldness, we take hold of the access we have to God right where we are. Fear tries to eject us out of waiting by convincing us to take matters into our own hands and shortcut the process. Instead, we can choose to remain planted and steady upon our waiting ground and believe that God will accomplish in and through us everything he has promised. We can resist allowing experiences and circumstances to define who we are and rather be anchored in the identity spoken over us by God's affirming voice.

As the writer of Hebrews says, "We who have fled to take hold of the hope offered to us may be greatly encouraged. We have this hope as an anchor for the soul, firm and secure." (Hebrews 6:18-19 NIV)

We who have fled. Fled to what or to whom? Fled to God's presence with us in the storm. We are those who are anchored, strong and secure. Not moving. Stationed, rooted, and grounded. Just as an anchor keeps a boat in place during rough waters, so Jesus holds us firm despite surrounding chaos.

This is the promise. When you rest in God's presence, you are planted. By the reality of Jesus in your life, you are anchored. The point is never to fixate on fear; the point is to access what is available to you despite your circumstances.

God with you in it.

With that reality grasped, there's a new way to approach fear. Instead of running from it, resisting it, or combating it with all your energy and focus, you can face it with purpose and clarity.

Fear isn't going to take you down; you're going to transform fear.

❧

Have you ever held a full cup of water and then submerged a golf ball, egg, or another small object into the glass? Water instantly flows out because of the addition of the object. Why? It all has to do with displacement. There is finite space within a full glass of water, so if an object is dropped into it then some of the water is displaced from it.

The same is true for us. The addition of love, God's love, into our midst drives out fear. They cannot exist together. John writes that "there is no fear in love, but perfect love casts out fear" (1 John 4:18). *There is no fear in love.* Fear and love cannot coexist. In order for fear to be present, there is a lack of love. This verse perfectly highlights the displacement relationship between love and fear. The presence of love expels fear.

When we experience fear in our waiting, the answer isn't to shame or force ourselves into a better or more mature state of mind. The answer is to welcome in the love of God. Then we can view fear as an invitation into God's presence. And taking hold of the invitation means receiving more of God's love.

Wondering if you will ever be married? Fearful you'll lose your loved one? Scared to surrender to God's leading for your season? Mess up the leadership role God promoted you to? Miss the opportunity when it came along?

Instead of being dislodged by fear, instead of disengaging from God, instead of separating yourself from your true identity, allow that fear to drive you into the love of God. He is love. He pours his love upon you. And his love is meant to anchor, lavish, and refine you.

❧

I love that as Paul goes through the armor of God in Ephesians 6, he makes it clear that you and I are to put it on "so that...you may be able *to stand your ground*, and after you have done everything, *to stand*" (vv. 13 NIV, emphasis mine).

Your call, as you journey through the waiting process, is to stand firm where you are. To move when God says "go" but until he does to wait securely that he has called you to stand here.

What fear wants most is to get you moving out of the place of waiting far quicker than you are meant to. It wants you to shortcut yourself from the process that changes and matures you. The danger in this is that if you move too quickly, you can find yourself in positions or circumstances that were never intended for you.

You aren't called to push yourself out of the season you're in. You are called to stand tall and strong on this ground. To not be moved by what is happening around you. To be secure in who you are and who God is. To be anchored to the truth that he is present with you in this place.

The most powerful response you can give to fear is to stand firm in the middle of it.

How contrary this is to the messages that urge you to quickly, forcefully, and urgently move yourself out of where you are. To control your destiny and fix your problems. But here in Ephesians 6, the command is simply to stand.

This kind of waiting isn't passive. It is active, fierce, and resolved. It looks a lot like I did with my outstretched arms desperately trying to keep my tent from collapsing in that hurricane. Waiting is about tightening your core and planting your feet, determining that you will not move no matter what storms may come.

Ultimately, strength and perseverance are only grown when the ground shakes. You become stronger when you stand as things around you shift. You become more unmovable the more things push against you. Transformation doesn't come when all is calm and quiet—it happens when things are pressing in all around you. The gracious gift you have in fear and chaos is the chance to grow by way of remaining firm.

That's no easy task. When you feel out of control and when your circumstances seem to be storming around you, it's difficult to show up and believe for yourself that God is with you. But you must look at yourself and determine that you are strong enough to withstand it. You can find confidence in this because you know who and whose you are. Not because you have it all together. But because fear offers you an opportunity to invite God to move and flow through you, enabling you, even in your weakest moments, to stand tall and strong by his power.

To show up for yourself means you aren't fixated on what is happening around you, but who is present with you and what has been promised to you. Pull your core tight, squat yourself low, and decide you will out-stand the circumstances. Out-hope the despair you may feel. Out-believe the fear that presses in. Out-wait the storm that crashes around you.

May you not move yourself out of the waiting even one second before God's presence ushers you forward. Instead, may you wait with resolve and determination—and so settle within yourself that in these circumstances, you will stand firm, hold tight, and wait.

CHAPTER FOUR

YOU CANNOT TOUCH ME

I was seven months into my year around the world when our group of twenty-five showed up to our hostel in Johannesburg, South Africa. It was evening time and we were all exhausted. The prior month we had been scattered all over Africa, so we were ready for a few days of rest before flying into New Delhi.

Given the size of our group, the hostel split us into two rooms. All the men except for one were able to stay together. Sixteen women plus one lucky guy gathered in a giant room filled with two rows of bunk beds.

After a quick dinner out, we went back to our hostel to wind down. In my room the women were all getting tired, which for us meant becoming quite delirious. We had reached the point where we were so exhausted that we thought everything was hilarious. And with so many tired people in one enclosed area, our room was full of excitement and volume.

After a long bout of laughter, I hopped up on the top bunk of my bed and dug into my purse for a pen to start journaling. Just as I did, our room's sliding door opened. My teammate Sarah came running in, frantic. With an ashen look to her face, she yelled, "What the heck is going on?" She bolted over to the sliding door on the opposite end of our room and attempted to open it. Not able to, she tried again to no avail. The door was locked.

She turned her head to look over her shoulder, which caused me to track my eyes with hers. Looking back to the door she had just entered, in he walked. Face creased, eyes locked, gun in hand. He shouted, "I will shoot you. Get down now. Get down. Over there. NOW!" He pointed with his gun to the area in front of the locked door where Sarah stood.

There are moments in life when everything freezes. When the normal and mundane are suspended. One instant, life is unsuspecting and moving about in a normal rhythm. The next second, reality is altered by an invasion of the unexpected.

Everything shifts by the entrance of one unlikely suddenly.

Those moments are the rare ones, sandwiched by the ordinary. You can't control when or how they come, but when they do, they carry an invitation into a greater depth of faith. It is the unplanned and the unimagined that changes us.

We all scrambled off our bunk beds and huddled in the back corner of the room. Before I jumped, it occurred to me that I was carrying hundreds of dollars in my purse to pay for our India visas we needed to get in the morning. As a prophetic act of believing we would get through this, I threw my comforter over my money-loaded purse before following the rest of my group to the corner.

Two more men with guns came into our room as the one robber kept yelling to us, "Sleep! Now! Sleep!" He wanted us still and quiet. Then he began screaming for phones, computers, anything of value. He wasn't finding what he was looking for and the longer his search carried on, the angrier he got. He ripped a ladder off one of the bunk beds and demanded we start giving him things. "NOW!" he screamed.

One teammate bravely told the man that her wallet was in her backpack by the front door and, if he would let her walk over there, she could give it to him. With a gun to her back, she made her way to her backpack only to find the pocket empty and the wallet already taken.

"Get back over there," he said. "YOU!" he yelled, pointing at me.

"Get up!"

In one quick move, I jumped to my feet and my arms instinctively shot into the air. I was doing my best to portray a wholly surrendered posture. Gun pointed at my chest, he told the rest of the team, "If you don't start giving me things, I'm going to take this one outside and make an example of her. Do you understand?!"

Eyes locked and heart racing, my mind flashed back to our training camp in Georgia. Just months earlier, under a big blue-and-white striped tent, a Sri Lankan woman named Shelvi spoke to our group. She told us stories of martyrdom, imprisonment, and forced exile from closed countries.

To begin her talk she walked right up to the front of the tent and asked our group the question, "Who here is ready to live for Christ?" Hands shot up. We were already resolved to leave our cushy lives behind to experience God around the world. Of course we were ready to live for Jesus.

Before people had time to put their hands down, she asked another question, "And who here is ready to die for Christ?" I purposefully looked at her mouth, waiting for a smile to come across her lips quietly communicating that she was only mildly serious. Nothing happened. Her mouth stayed firm. Unshaken. Determined.

Two things were clear: this woman wasn't playing around and this wasn't one of those "dying for Christ in theory" talks that you may hear on a given Sunday in church. No, this woman was serious about what she was asking. She continued, "If you are ready to live for Christ, then you must be ready to die for Christ. You must be ready to give him everything, your life included."

I have to be honest. My arm lowered a little, somewhat half-raised. It's not that I wasn't ready to die for Christ. Everything in me wanted to be a radical, leave-it-all-behind missionary. It's the whole reason I was going on this trip. I wanted to surrender it all to God. But die, like *die*?

In hindsight, it was prophetic. Not the dying part, but the half-raised-arm moment. I was saying yes to a faith that stretched far beyond the edges of my comfort or control. Because months later, I was now standing before a man who was holding a gun pointed at my chest, threatening my life. And as I took in the scene before me, a sinking feeling settled in my stomach—I may die tonight.

Standing on that burgundy rug with stains and pulls scattered every few feet, I caught hold of a revelation I will never forget. There in the deadly silence, I encountered the God of rest, the God of presence. It wasn't in the frenzy but in the waiting that I suddenly experienced a tangible, potent, and manifest wave of peace.

What washed over me was confidence, wild confidence, that my life was not in this man's hands and no matter the threats he made or the bullets he could shoot, I knew he was not in control. My teammates were down on the ground, there were several men in our room, and a gun was aimed at me when these words came to my mind from deep within me: "*You cannot touch me.*"

In this critical moment, I looked into the gunman's dark, sunken eyes. He returned the stare. All was frozen. Then he waved the gun toward the group and told me to get down with them.

Not long after, the men were out the door and revving their car engine to flee the hostel. Our group heard it all yet remained still, not wanting to move more quickly than we should. After what felt like an hour, the rest of our teammates burst through the same sliding door where it all began, their faces full of concern, anger, and relief. The minute we realized it was over, a dam of emotions broke open. Tears, wails, "shhhs" and "it's okays" flooded the room.

On that July evening, in probably one of the longest waiting moments of my life, I encountered the revelation that no matter what comes against me, it cannot touch the spirit within me. Because the spirit within me carries the supernatural power of God. And that can never be touched by the schemes of the world.

❧

In the most pivotal moment, I became utterly aware that the presence of God was with me. I was not alone. I can never explain all the reasons why things happened as they did. But I am certain of two things: I was at complete rest despite the threatening storm swirling around me and I knew that no matter what this man tried, he could never touch the spirit within me that makes me who I am created to be. Even if my earthly body were to be harmed, my spirit was untouchable.

The revelations we encounter in these paramount moments of life are the most threatening to the darkness we face because they strengthen the very foundation of our faith. We are never the same after we have experienced an encounter with the Living God. Whatever we believed by reading, praying, and thinking suddenly gains flesh, a heartbeat, and dimension. Breath fills what was once only information and makes it come alive. What we encounter, from then on we know is true in the deepest part of who we are.

What I experienced that night wasn't God's grace, love, or power, though I am certain all three were present and active. It was in fact his presence. His rest. The kind of rest that settles us to the core, revealing to us that God is with us no matter the circumstance. Wherever we are, there he is with us.

When we encounter God, rest comes. Not the lazy, tired, or falling-asleep-on-the-couch kind of rest. I mean rest that grounds us even when the storm is spinning around us. It's the rest that enables us to sense God. He's close, active, keeping us still. Such rest changes the atmosphere and creates space for God to move and breathe. That's what I inhaled that evening.

I knew I was settled. Secure. I felt God and I felt his tangible presence. It allowed me to exhale, keep my hands in the air, and look into the robber's eyes with confidence. I'm not saying my heart wasn't beating a million times a minute or that my hands weren't shaking from all the emotions but within me there was a deep sense of quiet. I was anchored by the truth that God was with me in the most intense waiting of my life.

In one breath of time, I experienced God as I never had before and because of it, I have never been the same.

I encountered Emmanuel. God with me, around me, in me, over me, and for me.

The word *encounter* is interesting because it comes with the assumption that it refers only to a single moment in time. In the context of encountering God, we consider it to mean that in one moment we met God and then in the next moment we didn't. The encounter takes place and then it doesn't.

In the Old Testament we read of such occurrences. In a particular moment at a specific time, God encountered one of his chosen people. God met Abraham in his old age and laid out his promises for what he would do for him and his family. God visited Jacob in the dead of night. They wrestled until Jacob ultimately left with a new name and a new limp, both fairly common to encountering God. There was God meeting Moses upon Mount Sinai, talking to him as a friend and imparting revelation for him to bring back down to the people. God's angel came to Gideon as he was beating out wheat in the winepress and told him to get up and do what he was called to do. There were also times when God encountered a collective group of people in which his glory came down and filled the place. The result was often that his people fell facedown because his presence was too much to bear, not uncommon even today.

There's no question that in the Old Testament people encountered God in intentional and unique ways. His Spirit was present for an instance of impartation when God called a person for his particular purpose. There was no collective filling of the Spirit for all God's people but an individual empowerment to fulfill God's calling. Like when God appointed Joshua to lead the people into the Promised Land, sent Isaiah as his prophet, or commissioned Jeremiah to be his mouthpiece.

God certainly appeared to his people throughout the Old Testament. Yet he visited more than he indwelled.

Then Jesus arrived. Even though the people had strayed from God's perfect plans, God was not done with them. He remained faithful to them though they had turned from, forgotten, and even blatantly disobeyed him. So God sent his Son who was the living fulfillment of God's promise to his people.

Jesus' message carried so much newness. From the very beginning of his ministry, he said things like, "You have heard that it was said... but I say to you" (Matthew 5:21-22). He challenged the entire religious system of the time. He confronted what the world thought about God and how to follow his ways.

He was the prophetic voice that ushered in a whole new realm of God's kingdom. It's why John the Baptist said the words, "He must increase, but I must decrease" (John 3:30). John represented the old system and was the forerunner who paved the way for the new system, which is the new covenant through Jesus. It was time for John to decrease because Jesus was here, and everything was transformed when Jesus showed up.

One of the new messages Jesus declared was that relationships were no longer about visitations but instead were about intimacy. He turned the way people understood an encounter completely on its head. You think, he said to them, an encounter is about an isolated visitation from God, but it's not. An encounter is about presence, friendship, and communion.

He began this message by saying such revolutionary things as: "Whoever has seen me has seen the Father...The words that I say to you I do not speak on my own authority, but the Father who dwells in me does his works. Believe me that I am in the Father and the Father is in me." (John 14:9-11) Jesus was saying there was no end to God and no beginning to himself. They were totally unified in relationship, purpose, and love.

Then he expanded the revelation, declaring that the intimacy between God the Father and God the Son was available to people through Jesus. "Abide in me, and I in you. As the branch cannot bear fruit by itself, unless it abides in the vine, neither can you, unless you abide in me...Apart from me you can do nothing." (John 15:4-5)

Jesus essentially said, *Make your home in me as I make my home in you. Dwell in me as I dwell in you. Have your presence in me as my presence is with you.*

Jesus was a walking manifestation of a whole new revelation of intimacy. And he set the standard for a radical point of relational access to God. No longer was encountering God limited to a moment or a visit or a person. Now it was about drawing into and participating with God's active presence among his people.

❧

Throughout the Old Testament we also read about how God promised his people that he would be *with them* in critical moments. Isaac was sent out to sojourn through a foreign land and God promised: "Fear not, for I am with you" (Genesis 26:24). Joseph was in the middle of a prison and there God was with him (Genesis 39:21). The words of the angel to Gideon were: "The Lord is with you, O mighty man of valor" (Judges 6:12). And Jeremiah, called to be God's prophet to the nations, was commanded by God: "Do not be afraid of them, for I am with you" (Jeremiah 1:8).

God was clear. Wherever each of these people found themselves, no matter their personal shortcomings or their inability to believe for what God promised, he was with them.

But just as Jesus' arrival altered the nature of encountering God, it also revealed the breadth of God's presence.

Before Jesus was born an angel of the Lord visited Mary. He greeted her with the words, "Greetings, O favored one, the Lord is *with you*" (Luke 1:28, emphasis mine). He promised her a child and told her she was to name him Jesus, for "he will be great and will be called the Son of the Most High" (vv. 32). He explained that the one within her would fulfill the ancient promise that "the virgin shall conceive and bear a son, and shall call his name Emmanuel" (Isaiah 7:14).

Emmanuel. God is with us.

Think about the words spoken to Mary in light of what we understand about encounters in the Old Testament. Mary not only experienced God in a single moment but here the presence of *God with us* was now *within her*.

Jesus' entrance by way of this unassuming woman transformed

how we engage with God's presence. It made him accessible to us. Emmanuel was born, the living and breathing revelation of God's intimacy at hand. No longer was God's Spirit merely a visitor of the moment. No longer was he encountered only by the unique few. No longer was God's presence about an experience or instance of time. As *The Message* translates John 1:14, "The Word became flesh and blood, and moved into the neighborhood."

That move into the neighborhood became permanent the moment Jesus let up his final breath at the cross, released his Spirit as a sacrifice of love, and then rose to sit with his Father in the heavenly realms. With that, all the promises of our abiding with him, his Spirit dwelling within us, and his presence with us till the end of the ages became reality. Forever settled.

God is with us, in our neighborhood. He moved right into our space and set up home.

What does all of this mean for our own place of waiting? When the realization moves from our head to our heart that God is living in us and all around us, when we settle into knowing he is with us no matter the circumstance or situation we face, everything changes. By this revelation, our waiting in the wilderness turns into the ground of intimacy. It becomes as great as the mountaintop moment of download from God's Spirit.

Every day carries the same weight and opportunity to experience God's presence as the super-spiritual and supernatural stories of Scripture. It is all ground upon which God dwells.

Whatever you are waiting on, hoping for, or trusting in, God is there with you.

❧

When I walked out of that South African hostel the day after the robbery, I was fully aware that the God I encountered within those four walls, the God who graciously allowed me to live to see another day, was going with me. It was never about the momentary encounter alone; I wasn't supposed to go back to seeing the world the same way I did before. The encounter was always meant for the realization of God's presence to change my eyes to see, heart to feel, and mind to think differently. It was always about the meshing of presence, intimacy, and abidance into a revelation of God that changed me for the seasons and journey still ahead.

When reading both the Old and New Testaments, it is clear that God encountered people in the waiting of life. Upon those desert grounds, when all was quiet and dry and starkly without, he met them. It was where revelations were implanted, identity was sealed, calling was confirmed, and character was developed.

God encounters you when you are stuck in the process between promise given and promise fulfilled. It's why he doesn't push the process along quicker than it's meant to move. Because he would never let you shortcut yourself out of the encounter that transforms you. What makes the waiting so powerful, as arduous and protracted as it is sometimes, is that it upgrades you.

When you feel out of sorts, wondering how in the world you got here or haven't gotten there, that's when God meets you. And not just for the moment but in such a way that you are different every moment after, charged with vision, purpose, and clarity in preparation for what is yet to come.

Before you move on to the next chapter, take a minute to pause. Close your eyes if you'd like and think about what you're waiting for. Consider how it feels to still be hoping for what you have not tasted or seen. Exhale the worry, anxiety, and troubles piled up on those shoulders of yours. Release the tension that is causing you to hunch over in despair. Shake off the lies that entangle, distract, and disengage you. Breathe out what you know isn't serving or empowering you.

Then inhale. Breathe him in, the living presence of God who is with you. Don't worry about mustering up the right words or the proper scriptures. Just take a deep breath and remember that God is with you right where you are. He is actively moving on your behalf and growing you in the middle of your current season.

Don't move quickly from the stillness. Give yourself time to be changed by God's presence so that the encounter you have here goes with you as an ever-increasing revelation of God with you. Let it transform how you see and approach what comes next.

Where you are, there God is.

CHAPTER FIVE

BREATHING ROOM

I'll never forget the sound of my daughter's first seconds of life. My labor with her was fast and furious, with my breathing becoming an issue at the tail end of it all. Eloise's heart rate suddenly dropped just before she was born, so the nurses were ready to flood me with oxygen in order to help me breathe. But in one final surge of strength and determination, Eloise was born and no oxygen was needed.

In the moment of delivery, the room went from chaos to silence as she was brought forth into life.

Like most babies, Eloise's first breath came with pitches and volumes that filled the room with the announcement of her arrival. It ushered in the noise that confirms life.

Up until a few days before writing this, I had never watched anyone take their final breath. But on Monday afternoon, I got the call that my grandma was dying. My mom, brother, and I boarded planes to Chicago in an effort to see her one last time. I sat in her room all day and watched as she worked to breathe, exerting way too much strength and energy to do so. Her chest would fall deeply then rise again, the rhythm of a woman soon passing into eternity.

It was probably one of the holiest experiences of my life. Sitting beside her, speaking to her, and praying over her in the final hours. She lived a full life and had a movie-like romance with my grandfather ever since they were sixteen. She loved God and his Word in a way I've not yet tasted, and purposefully built a legacy that continues on in her kids, grandkids, and now great-grandkids.

Minutes before my mom and I were to leave for the airport to fly home, we watched as she took her final breath. Her inhale and exhale grew fainter with longer gaps between them, warning us it was time. Contrary to Eloise's first breath, my grandmother's last brought silence into the room. All was quiet. She was gone. No one moved quickly or said much. She lived such a life of beauty that we wanted to honor the stillness of the moment.

Between the loud trumpet yell of birth and the silence of death, no matter how long the time may stretch or how short it may be, all of life hinges on our breath.

Because breathing has everything to do with life. To live well and fully, to be alive and alert, you and I must breathe. Specifically, we must inhale and exhale. Breathe in, breathe out. This is the rhythm that ensures we continue on.

❧

Though the breathing I'm talking about is of course physical, life also has everything to do with our spiritual breath. In order to live and carry forth purpose, we must remain mindful of exactly what we are breathing in and what we are breathing out as we stand upon the waiting ground. The beautiful thing about the inhale and exhale is the partnership that exists between them.

When we inhale a whole bunch of fear, we can be sure that we will exhale worry, anxiety, and control. It permeates our environment, our internal thoughts, and even our responses. We may not initially realize why we feel so concerned all of a sudden, but if we slow down long enough to notice, we can identify what it is we've been breathing in.

It happened to me just recently when Mark and our kids left to go visit family in South Carolina. The last few weeks of our lives have carried a heavy portion of real life loss, both in the lives of close people we love and those we're distantly connected to. Without even realizing it, I've been breathing in subtle doses of fear telling me to just wait until tragedy strikes us too, since it's bound to happen. Life has been too good for too long, so the lie goes.

This morning when I realized all three of the most important people in my world were together, away from me, I became terrified they wouldn't return home. Tears began falling down my face partly thanks to my current pregnancy hormones but more so due to the fear I've been breathing in while processing the losses surrounding us. I quickly picked up my phone and called Mark. Hearing all their voices certainly made me ease up. Yet still this morning is a perfect example of how quickly I can become panicked over a normal, un-concerning situation all because I've been inhaling worry without even realizing it.

The opposite is also true. If we inhale the goodness of God, the reality of his presence in our midst, and the promise that he is faith-ful to fulfill what he has planned, we exhale rest, truth, and power. And those all impact, change, and resurrect what is around us. Have you ever sat with someone who so obviously carries a thriving spir-itual life full of intention and intimacy? Their presence is one of peace and grace. I often find myself wanting to take a nap when I'm with these people, especially when they talk or pray. Their words carry an undeniable rest that has everything to do with what they have inhaled What is within them is flowing freely from them.

When Mark and I spent a summer in Mozambique, we were part of the missionary school overseen by Rolland and Heidi Baker. All that God has done through their lives and ministry to empower the nation and its people is truly supernatural.

During our time there, we would sit under this giant pavilion multiple mornings a week and listen to Heidi teach. She would typically arrive just in time to worship with our group. And each time she did, she would always go right up to the front, lay down on the ground, and immerse herself in God's nearness. Before ever sharing a word with us, she'd get low before him and receive his fresh breath.

By the time she stood up to speak, she was overflowing with his presence. Radiating with it. She shared her stories and opened her heart to us. And as she did, it was so clear that this wasn't someone who had just studied or read about God. This was someone who knew him intimately, personally, and with great hunger. Her words carried an anointing to them. It was only possible because she had inhaled God's breath that very day—and in those moments right before speaking to us—so that she could exhale the fresh, living reality of God into our atmosphere.

To release power that changes our surroundings demands that we first abide with and rest into God. The way to breathe out peace, life, and joy is to breathe in the real and personal presence of God. There is no counterfeit to encountering God. No replica for fostering true communion with him. We can never shortcut our way to releasing the fruit of intimacy with God from our lives.

There's something else that happens when we inhale the love and presence of God, and it has to do with the displacement theory I mentioned earlier in regards to fear and love. When we breathe in the fresh reality of God, it causes us to breathe out—to displace—our fear, worry, and anxiety. And exhaling what isn't life-giving restores freedom, power, and peace to our spirits once again. What we breathe in determines what we breathe out.

I've always loved the perspective John offers on Jesus' ministry. The other three Gospels are related, so they overlap to a certain extent. Mark was the first to be written, which Matthew and Luke then used to write theirs along with other supplementary materials. That's why there are some of the same stories found in all three, though they come with slightly differing details and additions.

The book of John is different because it shares an almost entirely unique story about Jesus. John's accounts were so powerful because he was a friend to Jesus, so he wrote from an intimate place of knowing him. In fact, John likes to mention that he was "the disciple whom Jesus loved" (John 13:23 NIV), which is a bold thing for an author to write about himself.

One of the stories that has long intrigued me is at the end of John's book when he shares about an encounter Jesus had before he ascended into heaven. After the empty tomb was discovered, Jesus went to where the disciples were gathered and visited them. John mentions that the doors were locked and yet Jesus stood among them (John 20:19), a detail that suggests he entered in a more supernatural way than just turning the knob and walking through the door.

Jesus greeted them with peace and showed them his hands and side as evidence of who he was, the risen Christ who had faithfully endured the cross. John writes that as they realized who was before them, they were overjoyed.

Can you imagine the emotion of this moment? Those who walked with Jesus for years, who were now fearful and in hiding, who had learned from him, lived with him, questioned him and ultimately left him, those very disciples now stood looking with their own eyes at Jesus himself. Risen from the grave.

I'm sure gasps, shouts, and praises all erupted in one grand melody of gladness. I'm sure there were looks of shock, disbelief, and overwhelming elation too. I imagine as their eyes beheld who was standing before them, their minds were racing with all he said would happen, all he said would come, and how loyal he was to what he promised. Jesus, alive from the dead. It was likely beyond all they envisioned, expected, or could comprehend.

Jesus then greeted them with peace and revealed why he was standing before them: "As the Father has sent me, even so I am sending you" (vv. 21).

Consider the slingshot picture we explored earlier and talk about people who were taut with tension. The silence preceding Jesus' entrance must have been thick and the waiting tense as they hid themselves away with fear and questions, wondering what they were to do now. Yet here Jesus was in the middle of their fear for the purpose of their sending.

Just as God commissioned the Son, so the Son commissioned his disciples. After recounting his purpose for the visitation, John tells us what came next: "He breathed on them and said to them, 'Receive the Holy Spirit. If you forgive the sins of any, they are forgiven them; if you withhold forgiveness from any, it is withheld'" (vv. 22-23).

Jesus breathed on them.

For years I have read this and wondered what in the world it means. It's so concise. There's nothing else said about what or why it happened. All we learn is that Jesus came to his disciples, said he was sending them, breathed, and then told them to receive the Holy Spirit and forgive people with it.

John, who knew Jesus so well, isn't spelling it out for us. It's a sparse account and to the point for a reason. I can imagine John saying, "Either you get it or you don't, but this is what happened." The brevity illuminates its potency. We can speculate that whatever took place in that room was so powerful that no flowery words or further explanation were needed.

Jesus breathed. His disciples received. They were sent.

※

So what does it mean and what does it have to do with our waiting?

The Greek word for *breathe* found here in John 20:22 only occurs in two other places in the Bible. In Genesis 2:7 God breathed into Adam the breath of life and he became a living being. And in Ezekiel 37 God commissioned Ezekiel to breathe life into the dry bones that were transformed into a vast army. For both accounts, the translation of the word has to do with bringing life into something that's void of it. It's creative breathing. It carries purpose, potency, and power to change the state of what is lifeless into something living.

When we turn back to John 20, it's clear that the breath of Jesus had everything to do with creating and forming life. He breathed into them the very breath of God in order that the disciples would become a new creation and go forward into their mission. The partnership of breathing—the exhale of Jesus and the inhale of the disciples—enabled them to release their fear and trepidation, which they had plenty of based on their context (vv. 19), and be transformed.

His breath changed them. They were filled with life that displaced fear. Now they could breathe out what they had breathed in, the resurrected life of Jesus. They became agents of life to the world around them because Jesus was the agent of breath within them.

What's so powerful to realize is that all of this happened in the midst of their waiting, while they were still fearful and feeling totally abandoned. There, in a despairing place, Jesus showed up. He passed through the walls, stood before his friends, and imparted the fulfillment for what he promised to them.

But this story wasn't just about sending and empowering. It was about faithfulness too. It was about fulfilling a promise in the middle of their waiting.

Back in John 7:38, Jesus promised that for the one who believed in him, "out of his heart will flow rivers of living water." He was talking about something that would happen in the future, about the Spirit that would later be received. In John 14:16-17, Jesus promised that the Holy Spirit would come, the Counselor who "dwells with you and will be in you." Then in John 16:7, Jesus said that "if I go, I will send him [the Spirit] to you."

All throughout John we read prophecies that lead up to the visitation of Christ from beyond the grave. This was the crescendo moment, the release of the Spirit from the Son of God to the disciples who loved him. This was the fulfillment of a long-awaited promise, and it came in the thick of their seemingly hopeless time. It came after death. When it appeared certain that Jesus would not show up like he said he would. When all was forgotten. This was the waiting ground where he was present with them and released to them his Spirit.

Following this exchange was the outpouring of the Holy Spirit in Acts 2. On the day of Pentecost, "suddenly there came from heaven a sound like a mighty rushing wind, and it filled the entire house where they were sitting" (vv. 2). Tongues of fire rested on each of them and "they were all filled with the Holy Spirit and began to speak in other tongues as the Spirit gave them utterance" (vv. 4). An unprecedented outpouring of the Spirit came with demonstrations of power and wonder in and through the disciples. It was supernatural and life-altering.

But before this happened, the disciples received the inner work of the Spirit. First they were immersed in life with Christ. Then the outpouring came from them.

When Jesus breathed, he imparted his empowerment. He gave his mission. He offered his people what they didn't have so they could do what they never could have done before. He changed them in the middle of their waiting. That's when the encounter took place, the Spirit was given, and his people were sent. It wasn't on the high mountaintop of their lives or their ministries but the hidden valley of fear, questions, and uncertainties. Right there is where Jesus found them and where they found him.

⁊₭

Have you ever heard the story of Chinese bamboo? It's a fascinating one. Chinese bamboo is mostly known for its surging heights, but what is rarely known is that—as the story goes—it takes years of inner, hidden growth to precede what we find so visually astounding. In the first year, the seed is planted and the farmer waters and fertilizes the ground. Every single day his duty is to nurture the seed hidden far below the surface. He labors hard. Even still, by the end of the year there is nothing to show for it. The second year comes and again he goes out each day to ensure there is enough sunshine, water, and nutrients. Despite all of his efforts, nothing shows at the end of the second year. Year three and four are the same. So much hard work and consistency yet no visual growth.

Year five begins like all the others and the farmer's job is as it has been. Nurture the ground, ensure there is sunshine and water, and wait. Somewhere during that year, in a five to six week period, everything changes. Out of the carefully tended ground, bamboo shoots burst forth that stretch up to ninety feet high.

Not only is the visual growth staggering but so is the subterranean root system. The only way bamboo can surge to such heights is by the development of a strong foundation over the course of five years. What can be seen as a period of nothingness is actually the process of developing what's necessary for life to be sustained and expanded.

Similarly, Jesus breathed into his disciples because it was the necessary inner work of the Spirit that preceded all outer work. It solidified that they were to live from a place of indwelling presence.

We want the movement to happen quickly but to receive what changes the landscape, we must wait. We must remain and grow in the hiddenness, and submit ourselves to the process that deeply and personally transforms us.

First we pause, inhale, and receive. Then we expand, launch, and exhale.

You, just like the disciples, are called to live from identity, destiny, and victory—even in the middle of your present waiting. You are called first to inhale the breath of God and receive all that is accessible to you: his joy, peace, presence, goodness, wisdom, kindness. You are designed to live from intimacy, from breathing him in. What you inhale determines what you exhale. The empowerment of God comes from the receiving of his breath.

And then the outpouring flows. It comes by way of the changing of circumstances, the fulfillment of God's promise, the provision of a pressing need, or the power that pours from you to the people and places around you. It comes in the middle of your waiting. And it comes testifying that you are not defined by your season but empowered by his Spirit.

This is the beautiful duality of the Spirit, the presence and the power fully at work within you. It is from this place that you move from a passive observer to an active participant. You encounter Emmanuel in the middle of your waiting because this is where you receive his breath, dispel fear, and learn to release peace over all that storms.

So may you inhale his presence with you and may you exhale his power around you.

Breathe him in. Breathe him out.

CHAPTER SIX

EXPECTANCY

When I was a little girl, there was only one thing I wanted to be when I grew up. Actually there were three, but I was equally open to any of them so they collectively became my single dream. For years I'd pick to dress up like one of them for Halloween. They all required the same kind of costume, which was helpful. Plenty of makeup, fancy hairdo, dress-up gown, shoes with heels—and I was set.

So what was my grand dream? To be a movie star or an actress or a model. Any of them would do, though the last one was crossed off once I accepted that I'd never reach the necessary height requirement. But the movie star or the actress, which I'm still not sure why they were separate options, that was my dream.

Given how committed I was to dressing the part, you can imagine my level of excitement as a fourth grader when I heard that there was a casting call in New York City. It was for a Touchstone film and they were looking specifically for girls my age. I was convinced this was it. They would meet me, watch me act, and sign me on the spot.

My mom was less enthused about the whole idea. While I was caught up dreaming of the shiny lights, fancy clothes, and glamorous life I'd be enjoying, she was weighing the reality of a child who wouldn't be enrolled in regular school. Or who would be immersed in a totally new and foreign environment from what either of us knew. It took a consistent level of begging over a solid week's time before she gave in. Just this once, she finally conceded.

That agreement was no problem for me since I was sure one

chance was all I needed. All those years of Halloween dress-up and dreaming were about to come true. I had no doubt.

When the day arrived, we hopped the train from our small Connecticut suburb into booming New York City. We had lunch with a friend of mine and her mom, who were also there for the audition. Then we headed to the casting agency.

We took the elevator up a handful of floors, walked down a long hallway, and entered a nondescript room with bare walls and bland chairs. Taking my seat next to the other young actresses, I glanced over my script one final time. While I had only casually read over it the last few weeks, I was confident my natural talent would compensate for any lack of preparation.

Finally, it was my turn. A woman came out, called my name, and escorted me into the adjacent room where I'd run lines with an actor of the film. I looked at my mom one last time before entering the room. I'm sure my face showcased my thrill and excitement, mixed with plenty of nerves too. Then I turned back, walked in, and took my seat.

The actual meeting was short, maybe ten minutes total. I ran through my script while the casting agent took notes. I fumbled more than I probably should have, but I also loved every second of it.

After my lines were read and a few questions answered, the casting agent told me that someone would call within two weeks to let me know of any subsequent steps. I left full of anticipation for what would happen next, ready to pack my bags and fly to California for filming the minute they called and told me I was hired.

Sure enough, two weeks later I came home from running errands with my mom and noticed the blinking red light on our answering machine. I immediately pushed the "play" button and listened to that same casting agent give me follow-up details.

"This message is for Caroline. Thank you so much for coming out to the casting call. There won't be any further callbacks at this time, but we'll be in touch if anything changes." *Click.*

My heart sank. How could they possibly say no? Given all my excitement, I was sure that this was heading in an amazing direction. Not being asked back never even crossed my mind. It was the first time I faced such harsh rejection, such a definitive no, and it pertained to one of my biggest dreams as a little girl.

Of course I could tell you plenty of other stories when something new invaded my day and I instantly stirred with expectation. I wondered what God was up to, how he might be answering long standing prayers of mine, and hoped that this could be it—the ministry, the job, the spouse, the wide open door. Yet, as much as I prayed and believed for that dream to happen, it didn't. So it all felt like it was for nothing.

Given the number of times I've experienced disappointment and hope deferred, I am convinced there is a flaw in the system. My system, yes. But the larger one too. If right at the beginning of God moving in a fresh way we find ourselves side-swiped by discouragement or, even worse, bitterness and offense, something is off. So what gives?

❦

It stands to reason that if the alive-and-present God who raised Jesus from the dead moves into your life, he'll do the same for you. When God lives and breathes in you, you are delivered from death. With his Spirit in you, your body will be as alive as Christ's! (Romans 8:11 The Message)

These words get me every time. I love the concept of an active God bringing us to life in reflection of what he did for Jesus. I also love them because in this passage Paul tells Christians to use their minds to unpack what is completely supernatural and impossible.

He says if God has moved into your realm and now fully dwells in you as Emmanuel, you can expect him to do with you what he did through Jesus. Use your logic, Paul says. If God did the impossible for Jesus, he will do it for you too.

To believe in God and his activity in your life means to carry expectancy that you will see him move.

Expectancy is intricately woven into the threads of faith. It's an outward expression of an inward trust that God is moving despite what you cannot see. But experience makes it tricky ground to navigate. If you're like me, you've encountered your fair share of stories in which your expectations exceeded your reality.

It's natural that expectancy gets derailed when the unexpected happens. When you catch sight of a hope coming to fruition, you are charged by the possibilities in front of you. Your mind races with what will come of this relationship, move, or new job. You begin charting the path for how it will all turn out.

But many times the course takes a sharp turn. Your vibrant expectancy for what God is doing can morph into disappointment as time passes and things don't head in your anticipated direction. The first date didn't turn into a budding romance. The job interview went nowhere fast. The move to a new city was sidelined just as you began imagining yourself taking the leap, living in a new place, and beginning a fresh season.

※

When Jesus showed up on the scene, people were expecting the Messiah to come and for God to fulfill his great promise for *hundreds of years.* All those centuries of silence from God and yet they were, as Luke says, the people "in expectation" (Luke 3:15). Even asking John the Baptist if the new guy might be the Christ they were waiting for.

I love the use of the phrase *people in expectation.* This was the ground they chose to reside upon. They could have been the people in disappointment, the people in despair, or the people in distress, but they weren't any of those. They were the people in expectation, resting in their faith despite how long and quiet it had been. They were still awaiting God to come and show himself faithful to his promise.

People in expectation are those who believe God will do what he says he will do. Their hope isn't attached to their circumstances. Their waiting doesn't diminish their expectancy.

Like I mentioned in chapter 4, we also learn early on in Luke's account about how Mary was literally expectant with the arrival of Jesus. As the angel greeted her, he told her that she would become pregnant with Jesus for "the power of the Most High will overshadow you" (Luke 1:35).

Can you imagine? There were so many things she could say or questions she could ask, but instead she responded with this: "Yes, I see it all now...Let it be with me just as you say." (vv. 38 The Message)

Her reply was a display of willingness and anticipation. She embraced and believed in what God had promised despite what circumstances, reality, and even human logic deemed possible. To walk out this promise, Mary had to step into an expectancy of faith and body that required every bit of trust in God to do the unimaginable in and through her. And she did. She carried that hope despite the impossibility of the promise. The result transformed the world for all of eternity. Life came from her as it had never been seen before.

She wasn't only promised that she would have a child while remaining a virgin but also that her son would sit on "the throne of his father David, and he will reign over the house of Jacob forever, and of his kingdom there will be no end" (vv. 32-33). There is no mistaking these words. The one she was to carry was the Christ, the long-awaited Messiah who would redeem, reign, and fulfill. Four hundred years of silence and God was about to break through.

And as God did, Mary remained expectant of his faithfulness in the middle of impossible circumstances. Though the world proclaimed *"no way,"* God whispered *"just wait."*

⁂

But what happens when things don't go as we want or plan? When our expectations don't lead to the outcome we're hoping for? The key is in the question. Because there is a distinct difference between being a people *with expectations* and being a people *in expectation.*

Expectancy doesn't always turn out the way we imagine or intend it to. What often happens, if we don't root it in the movement of God, is that expectancy can twist itself into expectations.

We are a people in expectation because we believe that God is up to something. But we veer off course and become a people with expectations when we start defining what he's doing and how he'll do it. If we're not careful we can put boundaries around what we're longing for, fencing it off with our guidelines for how it must be packaged and what must happen. We take what is full of wonder and stake it down with rules for how it will play out. We distort our expectancy of God's activity into lists and demands for him to fulfill. And when that happens, we exchange his limitlessness for our own limitations.

So the beautiful expression of faith while we wait, our hope for what God will do next, becomes weighed down by our expectations.

What was stirred by confidence in God is now gripped by our own control. Expectancy is a manifestation of faith, but expectations are grounded in fear that if we don't, God won't.

When our faithful expectancy moves into fear-based expectations, hope deferred turns ugly. That's when bitterness, offense, and disillusionment enter the scene. And because we unknowingly attach our expectations to God, our disappointment and anger become connected to him as well. With so many unmet expectations, all based on our own terms, we begin to see God as the one who misled, tricked, or failed us.

When things don't turn out the way we decide they should, we progress ourselves down a path of discouragement and defeat. All of a sudden we look up and wonder how we got here, in this place of disappointment, bitterness, and resentment, when we started out so joyously anticipating the potential of what God might do.

It's easy for me to grasp how the ramifications of this shift play out when I think about it in connection to my marriage. When I live in a place of expectancy for who Mark is, what he will do, or how he will walk with me down the unknown path ahead, I carry an excited freedom for him and us and our future. In turn he senses my excitement, which stirs in him a desire to wonder and dream, risk and dare.

But when I take that expectancy and make it about expectations—who he should be, what he should do, or where we should go—he instantly feels suffocated. What was initially an expression of love, delight, and wonder has now turned into a matter of right and wrong, win and lose. Now he has to fit within my predetermined boundaries in order to come out ahead. There is little life, freedom, or joy in this way.

For example, it didn't take long for Mark to learn that I love words of affirmation. When he takes time to sit down, look me in the eye, and remind me of who I am or what he cherishes about me, I am overflowing with love for days. But as soon as I put parameters around his words, I suffocate his effort. The minute I tell him what he needs to say or critique what he didn't, both of which I have done, the whole thing gets twisted. What was meant as a gift of affection turns into a game of control. Life is sucked right out of it.

So how do you remain in the land of expectancy without moving into expectations?

There is a way. When you are met with a promise or an unexpected arrival, whether it be a person, relationship, or an opportunity, your call is to ignite your faith without defining its form or time. Expectancy builds hope for what God wants to do however he wants to do it. To preserve your expectancy means to lift your eyes higher than what you can see before you.

Mary is such a powerful example of holding onto expectancy without creating expectations about how God would fulfill his promise. Her eyes were fixed far above the realities of her world. Her ears were tuned to a voice much greater than the voice of earthly reason. There was no way for her to know how things would come to pass and she didn't try to figure it all out. She received the promise, made herself willing, and waited in anticipation.

Expectancy is a part of active faith. It's rooted in taking God at his word. It's trusting that he will move in the middle of your day or season. In the book of Psalms it says that "in the morning I lay my requests before you and wait expectantly" (Psalm 5:3 NIV). Later in another psalm it says, "this is why I wait expectantly, trusting God to help, for he has promised" (Psalm 130:5 TLB). Laying your desires before God and resting in his promises, you are meant to trust and dream for what comes as you wait.

As you release to God what you hope and believe for, push yourself to the edge of your seat in anticipation for what he will do and how he will do it. Then, as you traverse that unknown path forward, hear expectancy cheer, *Don't be defeated by what you can't see or don't understand. There is something bigger to all of this. Keep moving, keep going, keep waiting.*

ॐ

Without a clue as to what I was getting myself into, I enrolled in a theological seminary in order to satiate my appetite for more knowledge around the culture and history of my faith. It was a season that required more from me than I ever considered possible. For four years I immersed myself in the nitty-gritty of Christian studies. I learned the Greek and Hebrew alphabets and languages, the history of heroes who lived centuries before, and the various stances on theological questions.

When I began, Mark and I were three months into marriage. Not a typical newlywed rhythm, Mark would head out to a friend's birthday party or some other social gathering on the weekends while I would stay perched at the dining room table in my pajamas, going through my Hebrew vocabulary or editing another exegesis paper. It was one long, arduous season of life.

If for no other reason, it was worth it all thanks to one of my final classes: Biblical Theology. I went into this class with a huge dose of senioritis, no surprise. But the professor, a true scholar who employed more complex words in a common sentence than any of us knew what to do with, began teaching about the overarching story of Scripture. The "biblical meta-narrative," as he called it.

This meta (grand) narrative (story) is the one God is crafting from beginning to end. Depending on how a person approaches it, it can be defined by a number of different themes. For instance, the overall mission of God to rescue his people, or the redemption of God's people despite their errors, or even the fulfillment of God's covenantal promises to his people.

This concept of an overarching movement of God throughout history brought such revelation to me. For the God who loved, redeemed, and called his people long ago is the God who is still doing it today. The God who was faithful in the past, parting the seas so his people could walk out of slavery and toward his promise by way of the desert, is the God who is still moving. Even now he is freeing us, transforming us on the waiting ground, and inviting us to step into the unknown land of promise just as he did for so many generations prior.

God is still speaking and still fulfilling. What we experience of him today is deeply connected to what he has done in the past and what he will do in the future. The end is not detached from the beginning. And right now, you and I are participants within this narrative. This is the revelation I experienced, that his grand story carries throughout all of time. When we remember this, instantly our eyes are lifted to see beyond what is immediately before us. When we perceive that God has moved, is moving, and will move again, our focus shifts from our current circumstances to God who is working in and through it all.

Partnering with his larger narrative means to see and believe that he is doing something right now. No matter how silent, defeating, or barren the season feels, we can carry an expectancy of truth and promise beyond our current moment. Just as he was at work in those who were waiting in the desert grounds or as they conquered their enemies in the Promised Land, so is he at work in us.

When Jesus was in the Garden of Gethsemane, waiting with

knowledge of what was to come, he prayed to his Father, "Abba, Father, all things are possible for you. Remove this cup from me." (Mark 14:36) Even in his despair and sorrow Jesus carried an expectancy for what God could do. He didn't demand it but continued with the words, "Yet not what I will, but what you will."

Jesus was able to endure a violent death because he remained expectant for God to be exactly who God was and to do exactly what he promised he would do. He didn't have set terms for how things had to look or when they had to happen. He participated with God in the process required for what was coming. He was open and trusting, surrendering his will and embracing his Father's.

Jesus held fervent anticipation that there was a story being crafted beyond what the hours prior to his death brought with them. He knew that the grand narrative required today, and also pointed toward what was coming next. He got through the pain and agony of it all because his heart was set upon what was ahead. "Jesus, the founder and perfecter of our faith, who for the joy that was set before him endured the cross, despising the shame, and is seated at the right hand of the throne of God" (Hebrews 12:2). His expectancy pulled him through. This wasn't the end; there would be a tomorrow.

As you wait and hope, trust and seek, stir with expectancy. Keep yourself free of expectations. How? By actively participating in the process of today. Realize there is a story being crafted from beginning to end and this is your day to play your part.

In the grand story that includes tomorrow and the next day and all those that follow, God's movement is always better than your plans, terms, or conditions. God's story is the one that continues you on the journey of freedom, rest, and promise.

❧

Mark and I waited a while to tell people we were pregnant with our first child, Eloise. Partly because we were in shock by the reality that we were actually going to be parents. And also because we treasured our season to hold onto this little secret of ours. There was life in me and no one was aware of it. No one could see it yet. I loved that we knew we were expecting when no one else did. It created such excitement within us for what was ahead.

Then came the early-popping phase when I had a small belly that confounded most people. Was I pregnant or was that an extra ten pounds? No one knew so no one asked. This phase was funny because, aside from a few close friends who knew I was pregnant, the world saw a potentially sticky scenario where one is wisest to keep questions to oneself.

Of course, it wasn't long after that I looked full-on pregnant. This stage constantly reminded me that labor would be at my doorstep in the not-so-distant future. By this time I had read enough to know that one of the worst things I could do for myself would be to tense up with fear about what could go wrong with my labor. Fear, it seemed, would increase my desire to control the process and could keep me from experiencing the kind of birth I hoped for.

The truth that resonated within me as I waited for Eloise was that the best way to bring forth life was simply to relax. Trust the process. Trust that little Eloise knew what she was doing and how she was going to do it. Don't control, don't fear. Allow this miraculous delivery of life, that was so much bigger than me, to take place through me.

No matter what process you may find yourself navigating today, be hopeful that God will move through your season and your story. Carry expectancy that life will come forth from you. And just like what all those birth books told me, be at rest. Don't force the process to look the way you want it to but allow the life within you to come from you at the right time in its intended way.

Whether you see or taste it today, God is moving and he is working. Allow yourself the gift of his story unfolding in and through you in ways beyond your timeline or limitations. Hold tight to expectancy and may it lead you into deeper rest.

CHAPTER SEVEN

MISSING THE SIGNS

When Mark and I first met, I was the stateside leader he re-
ported to while he oversaw a group of young adults around
the world. We would talk on the phone every week or so. He'd tell
me how things were going, I would offer advice, and neither of us
liked the other very much. He seemed arrogant, like he didn't want
my input. Truth was, he didn't. He was annoyed he had to regularly
connect with me and wasn't interested in fostering much of a relationship beyond our necessary check-ins.

Six months later, we found ourselves living in the same apartment complex in Georgia. He helped me move into my apartment,
which ended up being the same apartment he moved me out of eigh-
teen months later to marry me. I always smile at that fun little detail
God inserted into our story. But at this point we were carrying my
furniture in, not out, and we were certainly nowhere close to getting
married. In fact, he was dating a friend of mine so I really didn't
think much about him.

When he and his girlfriend broke up, I overheard a conversation
that had me believing he was now interested in my roommate. That's
fun, I thought. I'm definitely not interested myself, I also thought.

So when Mark asked me to go to dinner with him a few months
later, I didn't think much of it. My roommate was out of town that
particular night so I figured it was a "get to know the roommate"
dinner. Now, normally I am a fairly perceptive person. I easily pick
up on cues, love people-watching, and have a good overall instinct
for what's going on in any given room. If you ask my closest friends,

they'd say I rarely miss things—until I do. And when I do, it's typically a complete miss.

Sushi on Wednesday evening is perfect, I thought, giving me just enough time to squeeze in my favorite bootcamp class first. With no change of clothes or shower in between, I showed up to dinner in my sweaty workout outfit. It wouldn't have been a big deal if it really were a "get to know the roommate" dinner. But it wasn't. This was a date, an intentional time set aside to learn more about the woman he had his eye on.

According to him, it became very clear the minute I walked in that we were on two different pages. It took us another six months and a few more mishaps before he won me over. And of course when he finally did, I was his. But that first date, I missed it. I was certain it was going to be about *this*, but it was actually about *that*. My discernment was totally off.

Discernment is this big word that can get tossed around and it can be hard to know exactly what it encompasses. It's this grace-filled gift from God that enables us to receive knowledge, wisdom, and insight about what he is doing even when we can't see the complete picture. Discernment helps us tune into how God is moving the rudder of our ship. It clarifies the course of our intended path to ensure that we are headed in the direction we are meant to be going. Without discernment, we do ridiculous things like show up to our first date with our future husband in smelly workout clothes.

Discernment becomes all the more essential when we enter the waiting ground of life, surrounded by tension and uncertainty. When we recognize that God is with us in the waiting, we lean in to hear what he is saying. We listen to how he is directing us, which affords us the ability to move with intention and purpose as we wait.

In chapter 3, I talked about how the disciples totally blew it when they were with Jesus in the boat on the water. Jesus gave them clear direction on where they were going and assured them that their destination was set no matter what the journey might look like. Even when the unexpected came, when the storm was all around them, it wasn't meant to discourage them. Circumstances were never going to threaten or deter God's purpose and plan.

But the disciples missed it. They neglected the promise and frantically allowed fear to overcome their faith until they couldn't handle it anymore and had to wake up Jesus. They missed that Jesus was doing exactly what he was meant to be doing. They didn't realize that it was probably what they were meant to be doing too—resting deeply in the peace of his promise despite what was swirling around. The disciples added chaos to the storm by breathing in fear. Jesus resided in certainty by trusting God's plan without concern for circumstances.

The disciples missed that this moment wasn't for fretting over what was happening around them; it was an opportunity to rest in the greater reality of God's presence with them.

❧

There's another story that recounts when the disciples didn't catch hold of what was happening and what they were to do. In Mark 14, the disciples and Jesus concluded the Passover meal and Jesus told them he wouldn't partake in another meal like this until "that day when I drink it new in the kingdom of God" (vv. 25). Then, before they went to the Mount of Olives, they sang a hymn. It is tradition to sing psalms throughout the whole Passover meal. These songs come from the Hallel, which is comprised of Psalms 113 to 118. Since it is the last psalm of the Hallel, we can be fairly certain that before heading to the Mount of Olives they ended by singing the words of Psalm 118.

Imagine the power of this waiting moment. Jesus knew what was coming in the hours ahead and the last words he sang with his friends before going to the garden were ones of thanksgiving. He declared who God was and that his presence was with him. Then he closed with the words: "You are my God, and I will praise you; you are my God, and I will exalt you. Give thanks to the Lord, for he is good; his love endures forever." (vv. 28-29 NIV) With those words released in the holy space of waiting, the group continued forward to the garden. To the fate that awaited Jesus there.

Jesus then predicted that all those who were with him would fall away, including Peter. Though Peter adamantly promised he wouldn't, Jesus told him that before the night was over he would disown Jesus three times. Peter didn't have ears to hear it and was flabbergasted that Jesus would accuse him of such betrayal.

Then they proceeded to the Garden of Gethsemane, an olive orchard on the Mount of Olives. Once there Jesus gave clear instructions to his disciples: "Sit here while I pray" (Mark 14:32). He took his closest three—Peter, James, and John—a little farther away and revealed to them what was going on. Jesus told them, "My soul is very sorrowful, even to death. Remain here and watch." (vv. 34) Jesus' directions were simple and specific. In Greek the word for watch is *grégoreó*, which literally means to stay alert and keep awake. It carries a charge to be vigilant, responsible, watchful. Jesus' command was essentially this: *Don't sleep! Keep those eyes open and your hearts alive— and be alert in mind and body for what is about to happen.*

Then he left them. He wandered off alone and fell to his knees, praying for his Father to take the cup of suffering from him and offering his holy (and whole) surrender. "Yet not what I will, but what you will" (vv. 36). Returning to his disciples, he found them asleep and asked Peter, "Could you not watch one hour? Watch and pray that you may not enter into temptation." (vv. 37-38) Once again, Jesus was clear that this wasn't the time to rest. This was the time to stay awake and keep alert.

Jesus returned twice more, each time finding them asleep. His final words before the beginning of his arrest were, "Are you still sleeping and taking your rest? It is enough; the hour has come." (vv. 41) Then he told them to look and rise, for his betrayer had arrived.

It was dark and late, and they all had consumed a good bit of wine from the Passover meal. It's not hard to understand why the disciples could not remain awake for the life of them. Even still, they missed it...again. Jesus repeatedly commanded them to keep their eyes open and stay alert, and all they did was fall asleep. They forgot what was required of them in Jesus' darkest hour.

When the storm raged around them, the disciples were invited to rest and they didn't do it. Now in the garden, they were commanded to keep awake and wrestle in prayer on behalf of their dear friend. Yet still they missed it.

What is clear by these two accounts is that there isn't a blueprint to follow that directs us the same way in every instance. Instead, we need the gift of discernment in order to know what God is doing, saying, and asking for in the moment of waiting. Discernment grants us access to the present movement of God that is not constrained by formulas or staked down by expectations. It reveals to us what our response is to be given his current activity.

❧

Discernment is necessary for faithful and intentional navigation through our waiting. It enables us to know when we should be alert and when we should sleep. When we are to push through resistance, struggles, and obstacles, and when we are to stop, rest, and be.

The Bible is filled with directives for both. While some may think it means God doesn't know what he wants, the truth is that he is pointing to the need for both as essential components on the journey.

Let's say you are trying to discern if you should take the first step into a brand new career path or not. Do you wait for a door to open on its own or do you email every agency you want to work with, set up phone calls and lunch dates, and network your way through the process until you're walking into a fresh season? Or you've been trying to conceive for a while now and are deciding whether you want to seek fertility treatments or continue as you are doing and wait for God to move. Or maybe you are hoping to be married. You can keep doing the same things, like hanging with your usual friends and frequenting the typical places, until someone new crosses your path. Or you can sign up on a dating website, reach out to friends asking for connections, or say yes to every opportunity you have to meet someone.

These are real situations that come with important questions you've likely asked and the underlying one to all of them is, what do you *do* in the middle of the waiting? This is when discernment becomes critical and you cannot afford to disregard it. Because discernment provides you unique instruction for exactly where you are. There is no blanket answer to any of the questions above. And if I knew the details of your story, it would become even more convoluted without the presence and guidance of God's Spirit.

So the question we must ask is, What is God saying and how is he leading?

The storm showcases the seasons in which we are called to rest. Jesus was actively participating while sleeping on that boat. He was powerfully resting in the comfort of what was promised—God with him. Such seasons emphasize God as the one who extends good gifts to his children. They remind us there is nothing we have to do but receive the inheritance available to us by his grace. It's why Jesus told his disciples that "whoever does not receive the kingdom of God like a child shall not enter it" (Mark 10:15). Entering his kingdom isn't dependent on the work we do or how we prove ourselves. It comes by opening our hands and hearts to receive what God is freely offering us.

But there are also seasons when we are invited to advance violently and contend faithfully as we wait and wrestle. The Garden of Gethsemane powerfully illustrates this. As Jesus said in Matthew 11:12, "From the days of John the Baptist until now the kingdom of heaven has suffered violence, and the violent take it by force." In certain times, we are to push forward in order to enter into new realms of power and authority. Faith is not always about resting. Many times it is about wrestling for what has been promised and fighting for advancement in what has yet to manifest.

So it is both.

And as God's people, we have the capacity to discern the seasons in order to participate in his movement and partake of his breakthrough. What has worked in one season may not be the way God wants us to do things in the next one. That's why it is vital to listen to his voice. To carry the wisdom to discern when we are to wait and when we are to push forward. For when we have clarity, then we can partner with God in what he is doing right where we find ourselves.

❧

In Matthew 9, Jesus was speaking with his disciples when a ruler came, knelt before him, and told him that his daughter had just died. In the middle of a bunch of religious people, this man believed that she would be healed if Jesus would come and lay his hand on her. The ruler wasn't deterred by the fact that she was already dead because he recognized who was before him.

So Jesus got moving with his disciples through the crowd surrounding him and in the middle of all these frenzied people, there was a woman. My guess is she had been watching Jesus for a while, beholding what he was able to do by the power of God, and stirring with faith for what could be done in her own life. On this particular day she decided it was time for her healing. It was time for her to advance and take hold of her breakthrough from a sickness she had long endured. She inched forward, pushed through the people, and waited until Jesus would pass by her. Just as he did, in the middle of all the noise and chaos, she reached out her hand and touched the edge of his cloak from behind him.

What's beautiful to me about this moment is that Jesus didn't single out this woman in the crowd in order to extend healing to her. He didn't find and call for her. Instead, she recognized the healer and reached out to take hold of what only he could give her. She said to herself, "If I only touch his cloak, I will be healed" (vv. 21 NIV). She determined that a simple act of faith could produce massive freedom in her life. She took action, stretched out her hand, and touched Jesus. Instead of waiting for healing to come to her, she laid hold of it. She believed that today was her day for breakthrough.

Jesus, feeling the power leave him, turned and looked at her. Then he said to her, "Take heart, daughter;...your faith has made you well" (vv. 22). For twelve years she endured pain and bleeding. Yet in one moment of faith she resolved that healing was accessible to her and seized it.

The religious leaders surrounding Jesus were caught up in their outward demonstrations of righteous living. But this woman, forgotten by society and lost in the crowd, recognized the authority Jesus carried. So she positioned herself to touch his cloak and believed that the mere hem of his garment carried enough power to set her free from twelve years of discomfort and shame. She put a bold demand on the anointing of Jesus before her. She discerned the seasons and aligned herself with the reality of God with her. As she did, she partnered to release breakthrough upon her arduous season of waiting.

There are three vital components we can pull from this story that speak to the process of discerning the seasons. First, when it comes to waiting on God, we want to position ourselves for breakthrough. What that means is that you likely have to activate yourself and move to the right environment. Waiting for a spouse while hanging at home on the couch every weekend isn't the best avenue for meeting someone. Nor is failing to update your resume and avoiding the task of applying for jobs while petitioning God to give you a new career opportunity. It is crucial that you move yourself into an atmosphere that creates and stirs faith and expectancy within you.

Secondly, we want to see, recognize, and hold tightly to the power of the Holy Spirit made available to us through Christ. This means meditating on scriptures, listening for his voice, and recording his promises. Maybe you write them down on the mirror in your bathroom like I do or on a sticky note in your car. Wherever you keep them, constantly read over and rehearse them. No matter what action you take in the middle of your waiting, you cannot afford to forget what has been promised, granted, and made available to you.

Finally, just like the woman in this story, place expectancy upon the Holy Spirit to move and do what has been promised. God declares he will intervene on your behalf, do the impossible in and through you, and give you the gift of his Spirit with no limits. Carry expectancy that God will do as he says, whether you are called to rest in the middle of a storm or advance by faith against pressing challenges. The Holy Spirit has been given to you, resides in you, and is moving all around you. Wait confidently for his activity. No matter how many days, months, or years you have waited, you can still anticipate God to break through.

ॐ

So many people are stuck waiting in a passive stance that keeps them from participating in the grand story God is writing today and the days ahead. Remember, the waiting I am talking about has nothing to do with passivity. Instead, it requires activity—trust, hope, faith, and expectancy that God will move despite circumstances.

Waiting is never about sitting on the sidelines of your life, hoping you will be picked. Because the truth is, you are already chosen. You are already seen. You already carry the supernatural power of the Spirit through Christ.

Waiting is also not about believing that life starts when breakthrough happens. It doesn't commence when fulfillment comes. The divine ground of waiting doesn't align with the notion that your life is upgraded only when you receive what you are hoping for. Life is happening right now before you.

And waiting never suggests to do nothing. It means to be intentional. If you are in a season of resting through the storm as the waves and winds swirl around you, do that and do it boldly. If you are in a season of sacrificing sleep, friends, and comfort to petition God to move, participate fully and with everything you have.

Ultimately, waiting is about pursuing the fruit of the season God has planted you in. It's about keeping your ears open to his direction and wildly holding on to hopeful expectancy for what will come.

ୡ

Ten years ago I was living in South Africa when my friend Becky and I both had this crazy, mutual stirring that God was calling us to a forty day fast. With willing hearts, and no idea of the bodily struggle to ensue, we said yes. Only twenty-four hours in and I wanted to pluck out the eyes of anyone who held food to their lips in my presence. I would love to say I eventually settled into the fast, but in actuality I battled my flesh (and my growling stomach) every step of the way.

Around three weeks in, we went to Swaziland for a quick debrief with the leaders of our trip before traveling to Malawi. Upon arrival, we were asked to end the fast due to concerns about our health while being so far from medical care. Additionally, we were about to enter a country where it might seem offensive to hosts who wanted to demonstrate honor by offering us food.

For a girl who fought against the fast every moment of each day, you'd think I would burst out in songs of overwhelming joy. But in reality, I mourned the changing of seasons. I struggled to agree with the leadership's decision to end the fast we had so clearly sensed God leading us in. But we stopped. I didn't get it, but I settled into it as best as I could.

It took our team a solid forty hours to drive from South Africa to Malawi. Seven of us in a five passenger pickup truck was quite the adventure. Not to mention the roads, which were covered in potholes that we tirelessly tried to maneuver around. By the time we arrived at our hostel in Malawi, we were tired, hungry, and way too smelly. But I also experienced something amazing that evening—I instantly awoke. My heart was set on fire with fresh hope for what God was doing in Malawi. I was fueled by something greater than my own desires. A passion came to me from the Holy Spirit, powerfully stirring excitement and wonder within me for what we would encounter.

An internal revival ignited in me and, unbeknownst to me at the time, it prophetically pointed toward the external revival we were about to witness.

The next three weeks we hiked through wild hills and traversed remote roads. When our male teammate fell sick, the women on our team had a couple days of ministry on our own. We preached our hearts out with no notes or prompts except God's leading. Without question, these were some of the most powerful times of ministry I have ever experienced.

One specific evening our group showed up at a prayer hut in the middle of the remote bush. A group of about fifty were gathered to pray for God to move throughout their nation. The room was packed to the brim with people of all ages, from young kids who were hungry for Jesus to touch their families to the elderly who carried that same hunger decades into their faith.

Our group was asked to teach on the Holy Spirit and pray for God's power to be poured out over the people in the room. We shared about how God's presence was with us, in us, and moving through us because of everything Jesus had done. Then we prayed.

My teammate and I laid hands on a woman we didn't know anything about. It was clear that God was powerfully touching her, so we kept praying and agreeing with what God was doing. Next thing we knew, she was praying out loud in English. A woman who knew no English was singing praises and worshipping Jesus...*in English*. The only people in the entire room who could understand her were our small team and our translators. To everyone else she was jabbering away. In fact, even to herself that's what she was doing. But to those of us who understood what she was saying, we listened as she cried out to Jesus.

"Jesus, I love you Jesus. I worship you Jesus. I adore you Jesus." Over and over again. This woman was given the supernatural ability to pray words of adoration in a language she did not know.

That night was just one instance, of countless others from that month in Malawi, when God's supernatural wonders took place right before my eyes. Crazy, wild signs that changed me. Later I found out that Malawi means "fire flames." And how God lit me on fire that month.

Though God can and does what he plans in any season, I believe that the choice Becky and I made to lean into a time of fasting paved the way for a month of unprecedented breakthrough in Malawi. We didn't know what would come of it or why we were doing it except to increase our hunger for God. But we listened, we heard, we said yes, and we aligned ourselves with what God was doing. When it was discerned through our leaders and affirmed by the Spirit in us that it was time to end our fast, we entered Malawi in a season of feasting and receiving. Stirring with revival and passion, we were eager to behold the unexpected and unseen.

Discernment paves the way for breakthrough in your life as you lean in to hear God direct and guide you, and then willingly offer up your "yes" to do as he asks and go where he leads. Sometimes that takes you to the frontline of a serious battleground that you are to charge upon in wild faith. Other times it leads you into hiddenness and quietness, far from the eyes of the crowd or the adoration of others. Discernment enables you to access God's purpose for your waiting and understand how to respond based on what God is currently doing.

So what is the season God has you in? What is he asking? How is he leading you to wait? What is he calling you to pursue?

May you lean in and listen to him speak. Hear his whisper of guidance, affirmation, and purpose for exactly where he has you. Then follow as he leads, do as he asks, and reap the goodness he has in store for you right where you are today.

CHAPTER EIGHT

A SONG OF BREAKTHROUGH

I debuted my very first solo performance at eight years old. I was Glinda the Good Witch in my second grade musical and I recall that role with great clarity for two reasons: I was one of only two kids in my class to be given a solo act and it was the last time I ever sang in front of a crowd. While it didn't go poorly, somehow along the way I started to believe that I wasn't a singer.

It wasn't a big deal and I didn't think much about it...until one particular day in my mid-twenties. I was helping to train the groups heading out for their yearlong journeys around the world and some guests were in town for a few days to lead us in worship. They were full of spunk, spirit, and song. They swirled with these melodies and lyrics that offered healing, rest, and awakening to others. They were powerful and all I wanted to do was soak in their resonance.

One specific night, well past bedtime, my friends and I walked into the cafeteria where this small group of eight was singing. We couldn't resist staying. Their songs were like nothing I had ever heard. As the group sang out their swirling melodies, one person would release their own word or lyric that the others would then take hold of and build upon. It was this unreal symphony of individuals climbing together to higher heights and deeper depths of worship.

I stood in the middle of the room with my eyes closed and hands out in an earnest posture to receive what was being stirred. Caught up in the moment, I felt two hands rest upon my shoulders. One of the members of the group began to sing over me. His sounds were full of God's presence, possibility, and promise. Then he sang a piercing question to me: "Who ever told you that you couldn't sing?"

I stood there, frozen. Struck by what he asked. He didn't know me at all. How could he know that I had been told, or had decided, that I didn't sing?

I wrestled with that question for the remainder of the week. I wondered what God was speaking to me through it. When had I first determined that I wouldn't sing for others?

One year later I joined a four-month church program on the supernatural and creative arts. Because of what happened that night in the cafeteria, I was seeking opportunities to stir fresh inspiration in my life. This school had come at the perfect time. There were about forty of us that met every Wednesday evening, mostly artists of some kind. They were worship leaders with incredible voices hoping to record their next album, painters, actors, and a whole conglomeration of others with creativity oozing from them.

Then there was me. The girl who majored in math. The one who had just started wondering for the first time in decades if *maybe* there was more inside of her than the self-taught, self-accepted facts that said she didn't create or make art. I was so unsure of myself in the creative realm, but I was also ready to wake up whatever was sleeping inside of me.

On the first night of class, they announced that each of us would do a final project at the end of the semester and perform for our fellow students. "Get out of your comfort zone," the leader told us. "Do something you've never done before or present your craft in a whole new way. Stretch and push yourself beyond what you know."

Immediately it was clear to me what I was to do. By semester's end I would perform in front of this group and I needed to sing. The time had come for me to confront my fear. I knew the only way to combat the lie that I wasn't a singer was, in fact, to sing—and to do it in front of all these artists. My heartbeat sped up a thousand times faster and my hands grew sweaty in the moment of decision, all signs that this was God's prompting.

❦

Breakthrough often comes by way of challenging the lies that take up root in the middle of our waiting. No longer ignoring their presence or refusing to accept their reality, but instead bravely identifying, surveying, and wrestling them down by the power of God at work in us.

As we seek to encounter God, we must be aware that opposition will do what it can to squelch us by fear, disrupt us by accusations, and pull us away from where we are meant to stand. All these lies are attempting to influence our identity. To speak into who we are in light of our waiting so that we believe ourselves incapable to traverse the season we are in.

Through the storms I have weathered, I've discovered that I am most easily affected by worry and discouragement when I accept whatever lie is speaking loudest to me, whether it is that I am inadequate, forgotten, or unrepairable. The storms that brew around us as we wait, hope, and trust always have at their center one or more untruths. Those lies try to toss us out of our waiting and into chaos, confusion, and anxiety. If they can get us to believe in them, then they can begin to disrupt and dislodge us.

For most of us, there's a particular area we struggle with. There's a certain lie we seem to constantly combat, though it's different for everyone. If you briefly consider your closest friends, you'll understand what I mean. You likely have friends who deal with something that isn't at all a persistent issue of yours. Time and again you listen to them process their fears or help get them back on course while wondering how this one area keeps affecting them. Their concern rarely crosses your mind. You hear their dilemma, but you don't get it.

The flip side is just as true. There's something you wrestle with that those close friends don't resonate with at all. Every time you rehash your worries, you watch as they listen with love but little understanding for your struggle.

While it can be easier to pinpoint the fear in others, and harder to identify it in our own lives, I'm convinced we all have a central lie we face. We all have a fear or thought that acts just like our funny bone, easily causing pain and chaos the minute it is hit.

Given this, let's talk about some of the specific and common lies we hear and wrestle with in the waiting.

⅔

For me, the storms in my life often center on rejection. When I'm spinning most, it's because I'm beginning to believe I don't belong, don't fit in, won't be chosen, or am simply forgotten. All those thoughts focus on the falsity that I'm unwelcome and uninvited.

If I'm not intentional and proactive, it can take only a couple potent thoughts to ignite the questions once again. I wonder what's wrong with me or why everyone else seems to have whatever I lack. I can easily mull over words centered on myself, what I don't have, and why I won't ever obtain. They disqualify and deject me. And they always culminate in the same conclusion, that I should eject myself out of my waiting season before it rejects me.

For those prone to rejection, there are two common responses when the storms come brewing. One is to flee and escape right out of the waiting. The other is to fight your way through it come hell or high water. To remain unwilling to admit weakness or ask for help because fear says that such things would only confirm your deep inadequacy.

If you're a fighter, then you often approach fear headfirst, with way more determination and grit than necessary or healthy. You resolve to change your circumstances no matter what is required. You refuse to take no or not yet as an answer to your waiting. You throw punches at an unmoving wall because you believe waiting longer for what you hope for will validate your fears. Specifically, the fears that you are forgettable, overlooked, inadequate, or not chosen.

If you tend to flee, then you choose to forego effort and run in the opposite direction of your greatest dreams. You think it's easier to not hope at all than to admit that it didn't happen once again. Maintaining control over your exit, even from something you deeply desire, oftentimes feels easier to accept and endure. This way you can believe that whatever comes, it is by your choice and no one else's. So you reject yourself before anyone else can touch, hurt, or do it for you.

Rejection is especially difficult to confront when waiting. When you are fully aware that there is something you long for and do not have, you are exposed, vulnerable, and totally unable to control your outcome. In a place designed to transform and send you, how easy it can be for fear to inundate you with doubt and self-condemnation.

I know the lies of rejection well because of how personal it has been to my journey. I've learned, and continue to identify, my triggers and how to make choices that tune my ear to hear God's whisper above the accusations around me. But there are other lies that confront us in the middle of our waiting and it's important to mention a few of them.

૨૭

The second lie tells you that you are a victim, powerless against your circumstances. Like glasses with warped lenses, this accusation portrays a world where you are incapable to change anything because of the oppressive forces all around you. You're stuck, fear says, so no use in trying to move ahead because there's no way out. You feel as though all is against you, holding you down. Everything happens to you. Never because of you or for you. You are so blinded by your own experiences and fears that you cannot see how you've contributed to what is taking place or that you are able to do something about it.

When wrestling with what is still not yet, this lie tells you there is nothing you can do. Waiting then becomes passive. You believe that you have no choice other than to sulk, moan, complain, and sit by hoping that maybe one day things will change. What a boring way to traverse the waiting ground. Yet you can easily surrender yourself to this false reality and sideline yourself from participating in your own story.

If you are currently stuck seeing yourself as the victim, then you're not very fun to be around either. You likely seize any opportunity to tell your story of how life isn't fair and everything happening to you is out of your control. While anybody can occasionally slip into this thought process, and not with much difficulty, only if you identify yourself as the perpetual victim will you constantly complain and cast blame elsewhere. By this lie, you inadvertently believe there is no power in or available to you, so you are helpless against all that happens to you.

૨૭

Since I'm speaking bluntly, here's another prominent lie that gets highlighted when waiting: the belief that there is always lack and never enough.

When attention is given to this lie, you see the world around you differently. Suddenly, those who were your greatest cheerleaders and closest confidants now become the people who are taking or keeping things from you. Whatever everyone else has or receives only validates what you cannot have for yourself.

The powerful testimony of others is designed to promote faith and expectation in you that the God who came through for them can do the same for you. Celebrating the victories of others is one of the most effective ways to pursue breakthrough when you find yourself waiting. But when all you see is what you do not have and what everyone else does, you believe that another friend's breakthrough robs you of your own. A victory for someone else becomes a loss for you because everything is in limited supply. By this false perception, jealousy and comparison run wild in your mind and, ultimately, pour out of your life.

With eyes overshadowed by the belief that there is only a finite supply of God's blessings, you can respond in a couple of ways. One is to give up all together and become more defeated by each pronouncement of victory and breakthrough in the lives of those around you. Another is to compete fiercely, pushing, striving, and doing all you can to grab hold of what you want before the supply runs out. Friends become threats instead of companions. Everything is an opportunity to win. You have no ability to rest, since doing so would ineffectively channel energy and further delay you from acquiring whatever you must get your hands on.

※

The next prominent lie is that in your hiddenness, which naturally arises at one point or another as you traverse the waiting ground, you are sidelined. You equate hiddenness with not being seen, which speaks directly to your identity. You believe that if you had value to offer, people would see and commend you. If you carried purpose, you would be busy doing it. You become consumed by the notion that any level of hiddenness is wasted time, misdirected steps, or an unnecessary pitstop. So you begin to perceive hiddenness as something to be overcome or corrected. Your voracious appetite for the world's validation only stirs in you the urgency of your own movement into the limelight.

The fear of missing out will sabotage your ability to rest in the middle of the waiting. It causes you to stir with anxiety and worry that you will lose what you once had if you are hidden for too long. By this thinking, you place people's approval of you far above God's working within you. You substitute character for applause and wisdom for accolades.

So you forget that the hidden seasons are where God does his biggest work in you to prepare you for what's ahead. You neglect the truth that things such as maturity, vision, and direction are garnered in the quiet places of life. They allow you to stand with integrity and faith in the seasons of being seen (and scrutinized) by the eyes of others. You forget that God's goodness ahead often requires you to be tucked away and shadowed by the cleft of his rock.

All these lies show us that fear will do what it can to take everything from us as we stand in the middle of our waiting. Fear steals. Fear seeks to dethrone God, disempower us, discourage hope, and diminish value. It aims to strip the truth from who we are and the power from our dreams so we are paralyzed, overwhelmed by defeat, and left with little idea how to keep going.

Why? Because when we know the truth, we are compelled to continue forward. When we grasp the Spirit's power within us, immobility isn't an option. When we hear the whisper of God, no other voice can redefine us.

※

Peter is a powerful example of arising beyond his circumstances to become who he was made to be. And if we're honest with ourselves, he was also a man we can identify with. He zealously followed Jesus throughout his earthly ministry and passionately gave himself to the cause, even though he often seemed to have no clue what was going on.

In Matthew 16, Jesus asked who people said he was. They gave their replies and Jesus got specific: "But what about you?...Who do you say I am?" (vv. 15 NIV) I've always wondered if Jesus scanned the crowd and then intentionally locked eyes with Peter. Considering what Jesus asked, Peter responded with the words, "You are the Christ, the Son of the living God" (vv. 16). For a man who didn't always get it right, he sure nailed it here.

Jesus then spoke blessings upon Peter because he knew this response did not come to him by man's wisdom or knowledge but by revelation alone. Peter's pronouncement opened an understanding and intimacy with Jesus that none of the others in the crowd possessed.

What came next was just as powerful because, after professing this revelation about who Jesus was, Peter unearthed who he was. Jesus said, "And I tell you, you are Peter, and on this rock I will build my church, and the gates of hell shall not prevail against it" (vv. 18). Peter's revelation unlocked a release of power and authority over his life. Prophetic promise and destiny were sealed into his identity.

How incredible it would be to hear Jesus speak such words to us and to receive such promises. And yet what a sobering reality. For in the same moment Peter heard the promise, he also inherited the process. There was no promise fulfilled in his life without the process that came with it. The promise required the process. Because the process would mature him to receive and steward all Jesus promised to him. He could be sure, as we can, that the process would cause him to confront his fears.

The question to Peter, as to us, is whether he would be defined by his process or by the voice more powerful than any forthcoming struggles.

Luke 22 says that following the Last Supper a dispute broke out among some of Jesus' disciples over who was considered to be the greatest. Jesus told them that it would always be the one who serves, revealing the upside down nature of his entire kingdom. Jesus then revealed to Peter what would come to pass for him. "Simon, Simon, behold, Satan demanded to have you, that he might sift you like wheat, but I have prayed for you that your faith may not fail. And when you have turned again, strengthen your brothers." (vv. 31-32) Peter didn't get it and adamantly replied that he would follow Jesus no matter where he went. Jesus told Peter that, in actuality, he would disown him three times in the hours to come.

There was no way of separating the fulfillment of Peter's prophetic identity from the journey he had to traverse ahead, trials and opposition included. The confrontation was essential to the man Peter was becoming.

Within hours of Jesus being arrested, Peter denied him three times just as Jesus said he would. When the rooster crowed, Jesus looked at Peter knowing fully that Peter had allowed his circumstances to redefine his identity. While hours earlier he told Jesus he would follow him to prison and death, now he was denying that he even knew him. Everything that was occurring around Peter, the seizing of Jesus and the pressure of those accusing bystanders, got to him. He forgot who he followed. He allowed what he saw to determine who he was.

If we aren't mindful of God's promises to us in the middle of our waiting, circumstances will redefine us. The process is never meant to reshape our identity but to bring forth what has been within us all along. What is taking place around us isn't supposed to alter us into something we are not but to transform us into exactly who we are made to be.

How often do we grant a prominent voice to what has happened to us? How often do we let what we are walking through tell us who we are? We determine ourselves purposeless because we had another failed job attempt. We decide we are unlovable because of an excruciating breakup in the past. We declare ourselves stupid because of words spoken over us from years ago by a teacher or parent. In all these instances, we determine who we are based on past experiences rather than rooting ourselves in true identity. We allow the events of our lives to define us even when they contradict God's voice over us.

If we're not alert and active, our waiting ground can become fertile soil for lies to take root and overwhelm us. It can be easy to look around, survey what is occurring elsewhere, remind ourselves of what isn't taking place for us, and give footing to those accusations. But just like our experiences, waiting does not hold the key to our identity. It is never meant to define or describe who we are, what we are called to, or where we are heading. Destiny, calling, and mission are affirmed by the word and presence of God.

The unseen is meant to empower the seen.

❧

The beautiful thing about Peter's story—and ours too—is that even when circumstances caused him to lose his grip on the prophetic promise and process before him, he still could turn back. Not only that, but he could return stronger than before. And Jesus made it clear to him that when Peter did, he would be ready to strengthen his brothers (Luke 22:32). Such a commission could only be possible if, through that turning back, Peter uncovered an inner strength that would enable him to empower others. What he caught hold of through the process would become his offering to those around him.

And Peter did turn back. He had a profound moment of reinstatement with Jesus in John 21 on the shores of the Sea of Galilee. There Peter was charged to take care of those entrusted to him and be enmeshed with Jesus. In order to change the world before him, Peter had to live from a place of intimacy with God. Jesus disclosed that Peter's life would never be under his control. "You will stretch out your hands, and another will dress you and carry you where you do not want to go" (vv. 18). Then he told Peter that his circumstances weren't for him to worry about. Peter was called to follow Jesus, God with him, and to encounter him along the journey. To be present in a process that would bring with it promises fulfilled.

This is sonship in God's kingdom. The ability to be exactly who you are called to be despite what happens around you and because of who is in you. The way for Peter to propel ahead was to rest and abide in Jesus. That is where confidence and intimacy, purpose and mission are found.

What came next for Peter was powerful. The Holy Spirit fell in Acts 2 upon the early church with many people watching, mocking, and thinking they were drunk. The Peter of earlier days would have shied away from owning who he was among them. But now Peter stood up, raised his voice, and addressed the whole religious crowd. He looked right into the eyes of those who opposed him and confronted them with his truth. He released a prophetic word about God pouring out his Spirit upon all flesh as he had promised long ago, declaring who God was for them in that moment and in that place.

Following that, Peter's internal reality began releasing from him to influence his external atmosphere. Circumstances no longer defined him. Now he was transforming realms around him. Acts 3 says that Peter healed a crippled beggar and filled people with wonder because of what God was doing through him. His boldness and courage showcased that he had been with Jesus (Acts 4:13). And it was his shadow, *his shadow*, that people were trying to have fall on their sick to heal them (Acts 5:15-16).

Peter transformed from a man defined by the opposition surrounding him to a man changing the atmosphere around him. The process brought forth who he was called to be.

~

Waiting will always require our willingness to engage the process. And our process will call for us to overcome struggles, obstacles, and lies. So how will we navigate it? What or who will carry the voice of identity over our lives? Where will we live and rest from as we traverse the difficult parts of the journey?

While we can spin and strive to fix our way out of the waiting, there is a better opportunity for us. The chance to press into the struggle. To confront the lies that threaten our holy identity. And to become who God has made us to be.

※

Those four months of my creative school flew by faster than I was prepared for. Once I had determined to face the lie that I wasn't a singer, I recruited some close friends to help me. My friend Braedon lent me a guitar, taught me a few basic chords, and got me strumming somewhat successfully. Then I went about writing the words I would sing. I knew the whole performance was about way more than checking something off the list, so I was intentional about writing lyrics that matched up with the breakthrough I was seeking.

Then the scariest part came, which was gathering my friends to actually listen to me sing. Given my nerves, I knew I needed a few test runs before my final performance. Mark happened to be there for one of those impromptu singing sessions. We were still in the early—and awkward—phase of our friendship so it wasn't my first choice at the time but a sweet detail all these years later.

Finally the day arrived. I sat in the audience and watched as each performer got up to release their unique creative expression. I consciously had to silence that voice whispering to me that I was about to humiliate myself given how talented everyone else was. Then the leader called my name.

I walked up to the front of the room equal parts convinced I was about to collapse from the pressure and confident that God was about to do something unimaginable through my imperfect offering. There was a chair waiting for me, centered so everyone could easily see me. I sat down with the guitar in my hands and the mic before me. And I admitted to all those exceptionally talented artists that I didn't know how to play guitar a few months ago and that this was my very first solo performance since my Glinda days.

Then, with nerves running high and heart beating rapidly, I went for it. I sang my heart out for a room full of people to watch and hear.

You know what I love about what followed? It was so imperfect. Out of nervousness I strummed way louder than I sang. One of the leaders kept turning down the volume on the guitar so people could hear the words of my song. I was offbeat, my fingers fumbled between chords, and my voice cracked more than a few times.

But for all its shortcomings, it was my breakthrough.

I looked straight at that pesky, subtle lie that I unknowingly carried with me for far too long and I killed it. I confronted it head on, decided it had no more space in my life, and walked myself to the other side of it. No one else did that for me. No one else could have gotten up there, nervously sang my song, and set me free. The only option for breakthrough was for me to confront the lie and stand above it.

⇜

What lies linger over you in your waiting? What are the harmful words, subtle or overt, that have resided in your life for far too long? What is keeping you from becoming all you are meant to be?

You are brave and daring and empowered to look at what is holding you down and decide that it has no right to any more space in your story. You are allowed to do something about it. You are able to rise above it. You are created to stand upon it.

Confront those lies, fears, and limitations. And resolve within yourself that no matter the song that must be sung or the discomfort required, you will go after it. You will choose to become all who God has called you to be.

CHAPTER NINE

BUT EVEN IF HE DOESN'T

Back at the time of my Irish hurricane episode I was leading forty young adults around the world. If you had asked me then why I was the leader of all those people, I would have told you I had absolutely no clue. I felt unqualified and wasn't shy about letting others pick up on it. There were stronger, older leaders in the group with more charismatic personalities and flashier talents. Yet despite my running list of inadequacies, somehow I found myself overseeing this group of passionate Jesus lovers to countries in Europe and the Middle East.

Only three weeks into the whole leadership thing and my head was spinning. I was letting what people thought about me get in the way of who I was. I was allowing their opinions to influence my best judgment and squelch the passion that led me there in the first place.

When I initially decided to lead this group, I experienced an intense moment with God grasping the reality of what leadership would mean. I went into the season reasonably aware that it wasn't going to be easy or simple. To be out front and in charge of others can sound exhilarating, but it's a lot more terrifying when you're actually doing it. I knew I would be seen, especially for the work-in-progress I was. There was no hiding my fears or faults. Being so exposed left me unnerved and eventually in full-on spin mode.

My self-doubt skyrocketed and it seemed as though I couldn't make a "right" decision no matter how hard I tried. If I did something, I did it wrong. Either I wasn't clear enough to the group, I wasn't biblical enough for some, or I was overly spiritual for others. If I didn't do something, then I should have. After a few weeks of this, I felt so defeated that I began to entertain questions about why I was even there, thinking maybe my decision to lead was a complete mistake. I considered who would do it better than me and how I couldn't measure up. I dismissed myself right out of the position God had clearly commissioned me into.

One Thursday morning, fed up with all the confusion, I stepped away to clear my head. As much as I was dealing with self-doubt, I also knew the woman I was meant to become. I recognized the kind of leader God was calling me to be and believed that through this process, he was declaring I would begin to embody her. I envisioned the promise even though the process in between was brutal. So I went off by myself, away from the crowd and chaos, to seek God. I didn't want the noise. I needed the whisper.

I left the campsite and walked toward a cliff, thinking the view of the endless horizon was sure to pull my sights higher than my present confusion. Wind was whipping at my face and clouds were rolling in with force overhead. My mind was racing as my eyes beheld the powerful beauty of what was right in front of me. There was such a stark contrast between the insecurity that consumed my thoughts and the creativity displayed before my eyes.

As I paused and inhaled amidst the stillness, I became aware that there was no time for worries, questions, or lies to hold me down. There was no time to live a second longer in the spinning and swirling, in self-doubt and self-condemnation. God made it clear to me that there was simply *no time*.

There were forty people who were serious about following Jesus and somehow God had called and commissioned me to be their leader. This season wasn't about failure. This season was about stepping into the opportunity before me to give my life to something greater than myself or my fears.

Some of the most freeing words we can receive, especially when overwhelmed with insecurity or inadequacy, are the ones that remind us that wherever we stand isn't really about us. They inspire us that it's so much bigger than we are. And, if we want to participate in what is happening, we must raise our sights higher than our current horizon.

Stirring with self-doubt wasn't enabling me to accomplish what God had assigned to me. It wasn't doing anything for the group I was entrusted with. It wasn't helping people become more grounded in the movement of God's kingdom. It wasn't propelling me to become who God created me to be or to fulfill his purpose for my life.

Perched on that cliff, with the waves crashing against the rocks and the wind blowing crisp air on my face, it became clear to me. There were way too many opportunities to partner with God's movement for fear to distract me. Way too many people relying on me to hear God's whisper and walk in his authority. Way too much of my own desire for more of God's Spirit and power in my life. Way too much responsibility in this season of leadership to be concerned with how I wasn't measuring up or how someone else would do it better.

What a waste of time for me to be preoccupied with what I *wasn't* when God was so interested in speaking to me about who I was *becoming*. God with me was inviting me to shake off what was holding me down and keep moving forward in all that was springing forth—in, around, and before me.

This revelation came when I left behind the noisy crowd and encountered God in the quiet. When all was hushed I heard his whisper. There he reminded me to stay focused on his promises to me, the becoming in me, and his calling before me. He reset my eyes on where he was asking me to put my time—leading people closer to his heart, impacting communities through his love, and laying down my life for his kingdom to come.

That awakening changed everything for me. I encountered God's truth and it caused my perspective to radically shift and my purpose to be clarified as I continued forward in leadership.

Who cares about every way I could have been doing it better? Though self-evaluation can be helpful, self-condemnation doesn't get us anywhere. There is no end to that game. Because there is no arrival point to reach once we begin down the trail asking what is so wrong with us and how we can fix it. There's no "Aha!" There is just an endless trail with curves and turns that leaves us feeling increasingly disoriented with each passing thought.

What made all the difference to my group and to fulfilling my season well was that I was present, focused, and willing to become more of who I was created to be in the middle of the process.

How easy it is to wonder what's wrong with us or what we should do when things don't go as planned. Without even realizing it, we can traverse a path that completely derails us from showing up to our present reality. We can't afford to chase down every solution to our endless introspection at the cost of living today with purpose and intention.

I learned on that Irish cliffside that it was my choice how I stewarded my season and where I focused my time and energy. It was my choice to believe the lies and swirl with them, forgoing the opportunity to serve and lead well in the middle of the stretching process. Or it was my choice to shut off the spinning and be present exactly where I was, even with my flaws and questions.

My self-doubt didn't disappear in an instant, but it no longer kept me from participating in my season. Instead, I faced those fears and worries until they transformed into invitations to encounter God in the middle of what was happening. Waiting is always meant to draw us into God's purpose. It's an invitation to be fully alert participants, changing and becoming right where we are as we hope and believe for what awaits ahead.

How we wait determines *who* we become and *where* we go.

꿏

The early parts of the book of Acts share how the Holy Spirit descended on a group of people and filled them with divine power. The apostles began preaching with new boldness and courage before large crowds. The earliest communities lived in beautiful unity. They shared all they had, witnessed miracles take place before their eyes, and welcomed people into their family of faith each day.

But they also suffered. Apostles were arrested and Stephen even gave his life as the first martyr. One of the key players in this early persecution was Saul, more commonly known as Paul, who was vehemently against the followers of Jesus. He adhered to the law completely and believed fiercely in his way of righteousness. He sought to destroy this rising movement, even going house to house in Jerusalem and dragging people to prison.

Then something drastic happened. While Saul was on the road to Damascus and seething with thoughts of killing the followers of Jesus, a heavenly light suddenly flashed. He fell to the ground and a voice asked him the question, "Why are you persecuting me?" (Acts 9:4)

Can you imagine? You're fuming with hatred for those who are declaring Jesus the Messiah and out of nowhere a voice speaks to you asking why you're persecuting him. This is one of those encounters that leaves a person completely changed from that point on.

This voice instructed Saul to head into the city where he would receive more information. But as Saul got up, he realized he couldn't see anything. He was totally blind. This highly regarded, righteous leader known for persecuting the earliest Christians had to be helped into the city because he had no sight. When he got there, he waited for three days "and neither ate nor drank" (vv. 9).

Let's recap. Saul hated Christians and persecuted as many of them as he could. Jesus talked to him while he was walking along the road, blinded him with light, and sent him to go into the city— to sit and wait—for reasons Saul had no idea about. Talk about living in the uncertainty of the process with no clue when or if things would change.

Acts 9 continues on to tell us that a disciple named Ananias was called by God to get up and go to the house where Saul was staying to restore his sight. Ananias thought this was crazy because he had heard so much about Saul. He knew Saul was the man trying to kill people just like Ananias. But Ananias went to the house anyway because God had instructed him to go. He then placed his hands upon Saul and restored his sight. Actual scales fell from Saul's eyes. Following that, Saul was filled with the Holy Spirit, got baptized, and began preaching about Jesus.

Days earlier, Saul was walking along the road burning with anger toward those who followed Jesus. Now he was filled with the Holy Spirit and boldly proclaiming Jesus' name, all because God encountered him. It took one touch from God for Saul to be completely transformed for the rest of his life. But first he had to wait. And the waiting that followed the encounter is what brought forth his powerful transformation.

Consider how this takes place in our lives. We engage with God's truth or presence in a personal way but then find ourselves still waiting. While we were so excited about how we experienced God in an instant, nothing seems to change immediately for us. We expected the encounter to catalyze God's activity yet oftentimes what follows is...quietness. And, just like Saul, the choice is ours for how we live out and navigate the pause or delay that ensues.

Saul could have turned away and gone back to Jerusalem, continuing to persecute followers of Jesus and possibly remaining blind for the rest of his life. But he didn't. He went ahead by the direction of Jesus' voice and, following this dramatic event, he waited.

We also learn from this story that Saul waited a certain way. Not in anger or distress but in prayer. God told Ananias that Saul was waiting in this room for who-knows-what while praying. He was crying out to God and having visions of Ananias. The waiting didn't detract him from God; it drew him further into what God was doing. The unknowns of Saul's current season required him to be aware and alert right where he found himself.

Saul partnered with the instructions and plans God had for his life. They invited him to become exactly the man God had destined him to be, God's chosen instrument to reach the Gentile people. And it all began because Saul encountered Jesus and waited. From there Saul became Paul, the great apostle who spearheaded the release of the gospel to the far reaches of the world.

Paul heard Jesus and waited for God's movement. Then he launched out in power and strength to preach, influence, and offer his life to a mission greater than his own. The identity, calling, and destiny of his story manifested from his willingness to pause. Paul's encounter led to his waiting, and his waiting led to his transformation. Such empowerment by God required him to rest and receive who he was called to be before he was sent out to fulfill what he was made to do.

As I mentioned earlier, how we wait determines so much of who we become and where we go.

༈

Months into our marriage Mark transitioned out of his job working for a non-profit organization. At the time he didn't have a plan. Instead, it felt like this wild leap of faith that energized us by the possibility of what could come next. We were excited about the change and expectant for the new thing was God going to do.

The first few weeks after he left his job were so fun for us. We had enough savings to get us through a couple months without stressing so we enjoyed the uninterrupted and unscheduled time as newly-weds. We stayed up late watching a new show we were hooked on or chatting for hours in bed. We slept in long past the sunrise, dragging ourselves out by the promise of hot coffee and a slow morning. It was a season of wedded bliss.

But then the weeks dragged on and the resumes that Mark sent out weren't getting the responses we expected. Mostly he heard nothing, and the companies that did reach out to him for interviews never called back. Our season of quietness and rest abruptly turned into a time of anxiously wondering when, if, and how he would land another job.

As our excitement for the season—and our bank account— waned, so did our standards for his next job. At the beginning we dreamed of the perfect fit for him, the one with generous pay, a flexible schedule, and deep personal satisfaction. We prayed for one where he'd come home at night confident he had spent his day doing what he loved and making an impact bigger than himself.

But those expectations lowered with each passing week. Soon our best hope was for him to simply match his pay from his previous job or land an entry-level position at a company he loved even if he was overqualified for the role. Our season of anticipation quickly shifted into an arduous one of waiting.

In the middle of it all, I received a phone call from my doctor's office. I had gone in for my regular checkup a month prior and they had run their usual tests. Thinking nothing of it, I waited for those normal results to come back. But the nurse on the other line confirmed to me that this wasn't the case. They needed to run more tests—which led to a couple procedures—because they had found some precancerous cells that needed to be removed immediately.

It felt like one more worry on top of all that was already overwhelming us. We were weighed down by the stress of the unknowns. Although we were only months into our marriage, we felt like we had lived years of waiting without seeing much breakthrough.

One Wednesday morning I woke up feeling just as disappointed as the previous days of the past month. Yet on this day I decided something had to change. We could not continue to wallow our way through our marriage and current season.

"I'm done complaining," I told Mark over coffee that morning. "This isn't us. This isn't who we want to be. This isn't what we want flowing off our lives. We've got to make a change."

There was fire in my eyes that day. I was fed up and resolved that we needed to go about this season an entirely different way.

"I think it's time we stop talking about what isn't going as we want and start focusing on all the things that are." Mark agreed. We both cried. I remember the tears falling from our eyes and streaming down our faces. We knew God was calling us higher. He was leading us to do something different before seeing anything change around us.

We put on some of our favorite worship music, grabbed a couple pads of sticky notes, and began to write what we were thankful for on each slip of paper. Then we stuck them to our living room wall. They covered the entire area, from top to bottom and left to right. We didn't care how big or small something was that we wrote on those notes. We just wanted to fill them. We needed to remember every last thing that was good in the middle of our season, all that God had given to us and done for us.

That morning we made our first thankful wall. It was a visual reminder to us in a difficult season that we choose who are no matter when, if, or how things change around us.

On that day we decided that this is how our family will battle. This is how we will press into God when things aren't going as we want them to. We will thank him for what he has done. We will cover notes and walls and anything else around us with tangible reminders of how we experienced God so that we will never forget. And we will determine to keep waiting and trusting no matter how many days or seasons must pass before we behold God move. The length and difficulty of our waiting will not diminish our trust and expectancy of God's activity.

Mark and I will never forget that ordinary morning of newly-wed life when, in the middle of our disappointment, we decided we are thankful people no matter what. We solidified that gratitude is a core value of our family, for the seasons, years, and children to come. We remembered that we always have a choice to be who God has called us to be.

❧

There is no time to be lost in the chaos of the waiting season. Instead, the call is to remain focused on partnering with God in what he is doing and who you are becoming despite what may be happening around you. Because waiting comes with choice. You choose how you spend your time, what you give your thoughts to, and what you hold to as truth. You choose whether you will allow yourself to be defined solely by what is seen or to carry vision to see beyond what is before you.

One of the essential and active components of the waiting is the demand of choice, your choice.

When lack remains and time stands still, you are faced with deep questions of identity, destiny, and character. You may think such questions are answered when you finally arrive *there*. But the reality is they are determined while you are *here*, in process and on your journey. The breakthrough reveals that decisions were made long ago—quiet yet crucial ones—that led you to behold God's goodness.

Who you are has everything to do with how you show up to your season when the land is barren and vision is blurry. When all around you seems without, who are you then? What do you believe? What will you do?

The most powerful decisions come when you are faced with the ultimate questions regarding who you trust and who you will be *even if* you never see your hoped-for breakthrough. When your choices are only to ensure you receive whatever it is you long to have, then your dream has become your demand. But the powerful offering of the waiting is that, when pressed with such questions, you decide to continue to trust and move forward even when you cannot control and may never see. There you choose to value your becoming above your attaining.

In Daniel 3, we read about the beautiful offering of faith from Shadrach, Meshach, and Abednego. As King Nebuchadnezzar was about to throw them into the fiery furnace for refusing to worship his gods, they stared back at him and declared the words:

"If we are thrown into the blazing furnace, the God we serve is able to deliver us from it, and he will deliver us from Your Majesty's hand. *But even if he does not*, we want you to know, Your Majesty, that we will not serve your gods or worship the image of gold you have set up." (vv. 17-18 NIV, emphasis mine)

But even if he does not.

Even if we don't see the promise fully manifest or the dream unfold. Even if nothing looks like we want it to or imagined or hoped it to be. Even if all feels lost, forgotten, or impossible. Even then we choose where we stand and who we serve. Even then we choose to trust who God is and who we will be.

Choice is one of the greatest gifts offered to us as we navigate our waiting, for it catalyzes our transformation despite our circumstances. By our choice, we awaken, arise, and lean into exactly what God is doing right here and right now—how he is inviting us to change and become in the middle of what is not yet.

CHAPTER TEN

HOW LONG?

It was December 31st, 2014 and the clock was about to strike midnight. Mark and I were at our apartment with our best friends and ready to celebrate. We each poured our drink of choice and then stood on furniture to usher in the shining new year with our declarations of what would be. With glasses raised high and voices loud, we agreed that we would see dreams come true in 2015. I love any opportunity I'm given to raise my voice and loudly believe for what has yet to come, so our little huddle had me billowing with excitement. I distinctly remember watching Mark as he took his turn. With eyes of hopeful ambition, he held out his glass and boldly proclaimed, "This year I'm declaring a new job, a better job!"

The previous year Mark and I had trudged along with little breakthrough or traction. As ready as I was for a new year, we were entering it exhausted, tired, and disheartened. But being the optimist that I am, I believed this would be our year. I strongly anticipated that the arduous waiting, the stretching and challenges of the years prior, would transition into an outpouring of breakthrough.

It was a tall order for the beginning of a new year, but I was overflowing with confidence. I stood with our friends, let out a joy-filled "Amen!" to his declaration, and clinked glasses to ring in the hope of new promises.

Two days later, on January 2nd, I missed a phone call from Mark. I was walking to the elevator of my friend's building when I listened to his voicemail.

"Hey. Can you please call me back as soon as you can?"

Please. That word struck me as odd and out of place. We don't typically do pleases in voicemails. I rode down the elevator to the first floor wondering what could be going on. On my way out of the building, I called him back. He picked up before the phone finished its first ring.

"Hi." He was curt and quiet.

"Hey," I replied. "What's up? Are you okay?"

"No. I'm not."

"Okay...what's going on?" I figured the sooner he told me, the sooner I could fix it.

"Well, I lost my job. I just left."

My body swelled with emotion. Opening my car door, I made one of those totally confused faces as if to say, "I think I misheard you." But before I could ask him to repeat himself he capped it off with, "I'm done. I packed up my box and walked out. It's effective immediately."

"Whatttttt?" I trailed off. I was shocked. He had gone to work early that morning in an effort to complete some pressing tasks before we hit the road for a belated Christmas with his family. Both of us were struggling to keep up with what in the world was happening.

"Where are you?" I asked.

"I'm just driving now, not sure where to go. I may call some people to see if anyone's free to meet."

Good, I thought. A trusted friend to sit with him in this sudden pit of disappointment sounded like a wise move. But no one was available so Mark attended mass at a Catholic church, the only local sanctuary open to visitors on a Friday afternoon.

Today I laugh thinking back to that day. Not because it's funny, but because it's such evidence that our lives are being scripted by a hand greater than our own. Control and plans only take us so far until they fail us. If we give it long enough, life will draft up an act we didn't see coming. January 2nd, 2015 was one of those for us. We never envisioned he'd lose his job and it took us a long time to come to grips with what occurred. Yet the unexpected reveals that God's plans are loaded with intention and purpose beyond what we often comprehend in the moment.

That day also makes me laugh because we had literally just spent the previous five days going through Michael Hyatt's "Best Year Ever" course in which we outlined our goals, visions, and dreams for 2015. And I assure you, Mark losing his job less than 48 hours into the new year was *not* part of the plan. Already our fresh start had taken its first hit.

Later that afternoon I sat with a dear friend and shared about our day as tears streamed down my face. Full of shock and disbelief, I told her, "This right here is the irony of faith." What I meant was that despite our best imagining and planning, things rarely play out the way we envisioned. Dreaming is a beautiful practice of awakening our faith and soaring higher than reality allows. But while dreaming ignites, it does not guarantee.

Oftentimes we unexpectedly enter seasons that stretch us beyond our limits, bring us to our knees, prompt us to release predetermined plans, and draw us into greater dependence on God.

Mark and I began that year having just endured a long season of waiting. We were certain our time had arrived for breakthrough. And breakthrough that looked like something, namely transitions, jobs, and an influx of God's blessings. But instead what came our way was more prolonged hope and a heap of disappointment.

I'm certain our story isn't unique. No matter our best efforts for forward movement and future fulfillment, things do not go as planned. The unexpected disturbs every one of us.

❧

I've always loved the honest conversations with God found in the book of Psalms, especially the ones while navigating difficult situations. Tucked into Psalm 13 are words that resonate with me when I find myself overwhelmed with despair as I continue to wait. David begins the psalm crying out to God with the questions, "How long, O Lord? Will you forget me forever? How long will you hide your face from me? How long must I take counsel in my soul and have sorrow in my heart all the day?" (vv. 1-2) These are the laments of a man pulled and stretched beyond what he believed he could endure. Time was not quickening, circumstances were not changing, and his heart was groaning in agony for God.

I'm sure you are familiar with the emotions of these words. We've all been through seasons of believing that *this* is the moment of breakthrough only to be pulled deeper into waiting, hoping, and not seeing. So we lament like David, *How long, God? How long?*

In the midst of such terrible heartache, certain questions naturally emerge. What do we do when God disturbs our carefully considered plans, delays our hopes, or seemingly detains us where we are for far too long? How do we engage with our disappointment or frustration? What is our response?

When circumstances do not change and God does not seem to move, the lie whispered to us is that we are powerless. The deception is that there is nowhere to go and nothing to do. That we are perpetually stuck with no options available to us.

But when life isn't going as planned and dreams feel lost or forgotten, what becomes available to us is another opportunity—to offer a gift of costly praise to God. Because the truth is that we have our voice. And we hold within us the courage to trust and the faith

to believe. So we are always able to lift our songs of praise and gratitude to an unwavering God. Because thanksgiving carries heightened
potency when expressed upon the painful ground of hope-deferred.

❧

I was seven months pregnant with Eloise when I started looking for a
new rental house for our growing family. At the time we were living
in a cozy two-bedroom condo and I was itching for more space. The
rental market in Atlanta moves quickly, with desirable houses getting snatched up within hours of being listed. Given this, I actively
scoured every website looking for the right place for us to call home.

On a particular afternoon of internet searching, this bungalow
popped up in the exact neighborhood of close friends. I found it
within minutes of its posting, a sure sign it was meant to be. An open
house was scheduled for a week later, but I immediately emailed the
agent asking if we could see it earlier.

I loved it. My pregnancy hormones were high and I was certain
from first glimpse that this little house was the perfect place for our
family to nest. I quickly received a reply telling me I'd have to wait
until the open house, at which point they would review all applica-
tions and make a decision.

The day of the open house came and I went to check it out
with a friend. Walking through its doors only confirmed how much
I wanted to live there. The extra space, backyard, and cozy front
porch all wooed me with their potential. I envisioned our family
doing life there.

I submitted my application, prayed like a wild woman, called
up my favorite prayer warriors to join me, and waited to hear back.
A few days later I was in Ohio for a friend's wedding when I got the

call. There were too many applicants so they chose the couple with the highest gross income. It wasn't us.

In the grand scheme of life, problems, and letdowns, this isn't huge. This is a house we wanted to rent and didn't get. Yet my disappointment was real. I felt crushed by the news. This house made sense, I reasoned with God. It ticked all the boxes of what would bring ease and comfort, I reminded him. Plus I just felt it—deep in my gut—that this was our home. But even with my heartfelt petitions, which were many, it was a solid no.

I knew with a baby coming soon I needed to move myself out of that disappointed space and fast. Disappointment is natural and meant to be felt, but it's never a destination. It's an honest and raw stop along the journey that most of us visit more times than we'd ever prefer. But we're not meant to build a life or start making home there.

So I did the only thing I know really works when I feel most disappointed. I drove back to the house, parked my car in front of it, and prayed over the family who was going to move in. I still could visualize our family living in that house, but I had to accept that this wasn't our gift. I determined the best way to redirect my attention toward what was ours was to thank God for the family who would call it home.

With tears streaming down my face, I prayed blessings over the family who was about to move in—and for all those families who would come after them too. I thanked God for what he was doing in their lives and how he was pouring out his goodness to them.

Then, with disappointment still raw and real, I drove back to my cozy condo ready to make it the best home I could for our growing family. It wasn't my choice, but it was my gift.

When my daughter was a newborn, I read to her from this Bible for kids while she lay fast asleep on my chest. Every parent raved about this book so I thought it'd be a fun way to read to her the story of God's movement from beginning to end.

One of the stories that smacked me over the head with emotion is found in John 20. It's about the waiting of Mary Magdalene. The day I read it, I wept.

In the hours between Jesus dying on the cross and appearing to his friends again, I'm guessing the absence was eerily silent. Those who loved him most didn't know what to say, what to do, or where to go. How do you grieve someone who impacted you to this extent and was now gone? How do you mourn someone who was tortured, persecuted, and killed in the way Jesus was? How do you still believe in all he promised? What do you do next? And how in the world do you hold onto hope that you'll see him again?

His disciples and friends were utterly disappointed. They spent the last few years living with Jesus. They followed, believed, and loved him. Yet now he was gone. Was it all for nothing? For them to be persecuted and forced into hiding?

In the middle of their fear and questions, Mary Magdalene went to the tomb where Jesus' body was laid. I love thinking about her showing up in the dark of the morning to honor Jesus, maybe wishing for one more glimpse of him. In John 20:1, she arrived there and immediately saw that the stone was removed from the tomb's entrance. She ran back to tell Simon Peter and John about what had happened, specifically that Jesus' body was taken.

When they heard the news, the guys ran to witness it for themselves (with John humbly mentioning that he ran faster than Peter).

Once they arrived, they looked into the tomb and confirmed that Jesus wasn't there though his burial strips still were. John describes the linens as laying neatly and precisely on the ground of the tomb, a small detail that implies Jesus' departure from the tomb was more purposeful than a haphazard taking of his body.

Having seen it all for themselves, the disciples headed home. But Mary, the one who was there in the dark before anyone else, lingered. Even in her sorrow and confusion, she "stood weeping outside the tomb, and as she wept she stooped to look into the tomb" (vv. 11). Her disappointment and grief didn't cause her to flee. Instead, the tears poured from her eyes as she glanced once again into the empty tomb.

I wonder what she expected to see. To notice a detail she missed from her first glance? A hint pointing to where Jesus was taken? Or miraculously, somehow, to see Jesus just one more time? No matter what her intention was, this moment was powerful because even in her sorrow she chose to remain.

Two angels then appeared and asked why she was crying. She told them it was because they had taken Jesus and she didn't know where he was.

She didn't know. She was overcome with sadness because she didn't know. The uncertainty of the loss of Jesus, what was to happen next or what in the world she did now, it all swirled as it would for any of us. How did she make sense of this moment when she had no idea what was going on?

The disciples were hiding. There was silence and darkness and death around her. And she was carrying that weight of disappointment while having no clue where to go, what to do, or who to find. Imagine how lost she felt. I wonder how many of us know this kind of disappointment, the one where we find ourselves so shocked that we question what in the world we are supposed to do next.

As I read this story to Eloise, I wept because of the pause. The heartbreaking in-between moment of waiting. It felt so real to me. I don't know everything Mary was experiencing or what it truly looked like, but in my own way and in my own realm I get it. I know what it feels like to think things are supposed to go a certain way and then they don't. I understand what it's like when all of a sudden there's loss or despair so overwhelming it feels as though you will suffocate beneath it. I know what it's like when you don't know which way is up or where to go from here.

What Mary did in the middle of her disappointment is so beautiful to me because, despite what was happening, she didn't flee. She stood.

And what took place next was a miracle. She turned around and saw Jesus there, though she didn't initially recognize him. She thought he was a gardener. This small but powerful detail weaves the beginning of our grand story with God to its fulfillment here at Jesus' empty tomb. Just as our intimacy with God began in a garden, so its redemption finalized as the gardener stood alive and breathing right before Mary's eyes.

He then asked her who she was looking for and why she was crying. His question wasn't connected to *what* was happening. He was leading her to focus on *who*.

She replied by saying, "Tell me where you have put him, and I will get him" (vv. 15 NIV). She wanted to make things right. To tangibly do something, to put Jesus back where he was meant to lay and honor him in the proper way. She wanted to fix the uncertainty and solve the mystery.

But then he spoke her name and it all became clear. This was Jesus, the one she desperately wanted to find. He was right there with her. Immediately she turned toward him and cried out, "Rabboni!" (vv. 16) "Teacher!" She found him. She remained in her disappointment and he met her there.

Jesus then told Mary to inform his brothers, the disciples, that "I am ascending to my Father and your Father, to my God and your God" (vv. 17). Mary received her mission. She was instructed not to hold onto Jesus but instead to go tell the others what he was doing.

What strikes me about this encounter is that out of Mary's disappointment and uncertainty, she made the choice to stay. She probably didn't even know why she did. What was the point in standing by an empty tomb? But she knew it was where her feet were to be planted, so she paused.

In her waiting, she remained. In her disappointment, she stood. And out of it, she was commissioned by Jesus. She encountered him and he sent her forth.

Disappointment often compels us to flee, hide, or fear. It tempts us to believe that all we hoped for is now pointless. It tells us to abandon what we wait for because of what hasn't happened. But Mary Magdalene shows us a different path.

Disappointment is not the end of us or our story. It can be stewarded as a pathway *toward*. Toward what? Toward intimacy. Toward faith. Toward unearthing joy, life, and goodness right where we are in the mess of today.

࿎

Two years after not getting the house, we moved back to Atlanta after living for a year in Florida. I prepared myself that finding a rental property would be difficult, especially since we weren't residing in the city at the time. Mark was prepping me that the best option to consider was moving into an apartment complex until we got our feet on the ground.

The next day I did a quick search to see what rental properties were listed. I couldn't believe what I found. Posted just one hour earlier was the exact house I had desperately hoped to rent two years prior. Back on the market, available when we needed it, and priced at exactly what we agreed we wouldn't go over.

Mark called the management company to see what the chances were we could lease it and found out two things. One, they were having a hard time scheduling an open house with the current family. Nothing had been set even though they were ready to rent it. Two, they were only willing to rent to people who had seen the property in person. This meant that because we had seen it and wanted to rent it, they let us submit our application before showing the house to anyone else.

Just a few weeks later our moving truck pulled up to that same home. The one God gave back to us. Obviously the timing wasn't what I imagined—because it carried waiting, wondering, and disappointment along the journey—but the house represented so much more to me. The story changed and so did its meaning.

The house wasn't just where our family settled. It was where I had sowed prayer and gratitude even when I didn't think I'd ever step foot through its door again. Unbeknownst to me, the words of blessing I prayed in the middle of my disappointment for the future families who would call this place home were words for my own family.

Channeling prayers into what God is doing—especially when it is not the outcome we imagined—is a powerful way to steward disappointment. Words of thanks and honor are some of the best tools when we find ourselves most disappointed. They propel us out of where we are. They ensure we don't camp too long on the ground of what *isn't* but keep moving ourselves ahead by celebrating what actually *is*.

The home became this constant reminder to me of how much it matters what I do and how I respond in those in-between and not-yet moments. Those are what determine what comes next in the days, weeks, and seasons ahead. What I sow today, I will harvest. Not a single prayer, word, or tear of honesty, hope, or courage is lost.

I also learned that we have a unique opportunity to lift up an offering of praise to God in the middle of our disappointment. These praises aren't released only when we experience fulfillment or abundance. They are also sown and surrendered when there is fatigue and uncertainty. We extend such offerings to God when we are waiting and cannot see or taste or touch. That's when we are afforded the chance to thank him for what is and what is not.

And this is when we elevate our words above our surroundings. We lift our voices and sing to the God who is good to us no matter what, when, or how he moves. These words aren't anchored in what he does for us but who he is to us.

⚜

While David began Psalm 13 asking how long he must wait and endure, he ended with the words: "But I trust in your unfailing love; my heart rejoices in your salvation. I will sing the Lord's praise, for he has been good to me." (vv. 5-6 NIV)

But I trust, David concluded. His questions still lingered without clear answers. His sorrow was just as real as when he began. Yet despite all that hadn't happened or may never be, David closed his song proclaiming the goodness of God. He raised his voice high in trust, not only for what God had done but also because of who he was.

David stewarded his disappointment and despair into a gift of praise for the nature and presence of God. His eyes were fixed not on what was before him but who was with him.

Often the voices surrounding you can herald a message to repress discomfort and run as fast as possible from feeling sorrow. They can urge you to flee from what is disappointing and fix whatever isn't working as quickly and pain-free as possible. But that's not what David did. He didn't run from his emotions. Instead, he poured out his laments while releasing a song of God's goodness.

You can stand in the middle of what is real, felt, and painful, and there lift your rawest praise of thanks to the God who is with you in it. Because to steward what is before you—especially when it is not what you want, hoped for, or imagined—asks you to lift your eyes, words, and faith to praise who is with you.

As you do, your disappointment channels into strength. Your present lack upgrades to anticipation for what is ahead. Your voice soars with words of faith-filled gratitude for what you haven't seen. And your waiting draws you to encounter God for who he is.

So when you cannot see a path through or imagine a way out, can you still say thank you to God who is with you in it?

CHAPTER ELEVEN

LIVING BONES

One particular evening in Cape Town, I went with some friends to see a South African dance performance. Night after night the group would present an hour-long skit that showcased the need for a Savior. Then they would preach about Jesus and invite people to enter into relationship with him. Excited for a night out, our small group piled into a car and drove to the local school where the show was taking place.

The auditorium looked like a typical high school gym, with multi-purpose lines crisscrossing the floor. The walls were padded with a green vinyl that gave me flashbacks to my elementary school days playing dodgeball whenever it was raining outside. In the middle of the space were about a hundred chairs in semicircle rows around a makeshift stage.

The minute I walked into the auditorium, my eyes focused on a female standing on the other side of the room. She appeared to be about twenty years old with dirty blonde hair that was long and straight, and bangs swept to one side. She wore the team's black t-shirt to identify herself as one of the dancers. Yet what caught my eye was the brace on her knee and the cane in her hand. As I took notice of both, God whispered to me. While his words weren't audible, they were spoken to my heart and clear: "This isn't how it's supposed to be. I want to heal her."

From the moment I heard him speak, an internal battle waged. I kept thinking, "Am I really supposed to walk up to this stranger and ask her if I can touch her knee and hope that you do the impossible?"

What I was actually wrestling with was, "What if you don't, God?" Yet despite my fear of making a fool of myself, I was hungry for God to move through my life. And hunger is a catalyst that will propel us far outside our comfort zones.

So off I went to pray for her, with a friend in tow. Walking straight up to her I introduced both my friend Sarah and myself as normally as possible. Then I disclosed why we were there. "We actually want to ask you a question. We're both learning a lot about the power and authority we have in Christ and were wondering if we could pray for your knee. That God would heal it right here, right...now."

The young woman's name was Fissy and she kindly agreed to our request. She told us that she had torn her ligaments while dancing and wouldn't be able to rejoin her team for at least another month. Then she stretched out her leg so we could place our hands on her injured knee. And Sarah and I spoke the simplest prayer possible: "In the name of Jesus, we pray healing over your knee and all its torn ligaments. Amen."

I looked up at Fissy expecting a dramatic pronouncement of her healing, something like fireworks exploding above us confirming that God had supernaturally restored her. But instead, she gave us the sweetest "thank you" and said she believed God would heal her knee soon. We nodded in agreement, gave her a hug, and walked away.

Heading back to our seats, I asked Sarah why she thought God hadn't healed Fissy. I believed God *could*, so why didn't he? When we sat down with our group, we recounted to the missionary couple we were staying with what had (not) happened. "You know what you could do?" the husband replied. "You could test it. Ask her to take off her brace after you pray for her, just like Jesus asked the man to pick up his mat and walk."

His suggestion both challenged and inspired us. Before we could change our minds, Sarah and I walked back to Fissy hungry for God and ready to pray. When we found her, I shared our new plan with her. "Fissy, we'd love to pray over your knee again. But after we do this time, would you be willing to take off your brace and test out if your knee is healed?" Though a little unsure of our request, she agreed and we prayed simple words of healing.

When we finished, Fissy knelt down and pulled off her knee brace. With our eyes zeroed in on her next reaction, she cautiously put a small bit of weight on her right knee. Then, a little more weight. Then suddenly, she was standing on both legs without any pain. Before we had even gotten up from praying for her knee, Fissy was running, jumping, and dancing all across the room.

God had healed her knee right before our eyes.

I couldn't believe what had just taken place and kept saying, "You don't understand! I've never seen this before!" I was undone and blown away that God moved in such a tangible way through our prayers. Heaven came. Healing broke out. Wholeness was restored to her body.

God transformed my reality because I heard his whisper and declared his words. I was so hungry to see God's kingdom come before my eyes and it had happened, only fueling my passion and expanding my desire for more.

❧

During the few years I worked for a mission organization, I would stand before large groups of young people, mostly in their twenties, and recount to them the story of Ezekiel breathing on the dry bones. I can't remember when this vision captured my heart. But from the minute I discovered it, it became one of the stories I want to tell my entire generation.

Chapter 37 describes what happened to Ezekiel, beginning with the words, "The hand of the Lord was upon me, and he brought me out in the Spirit of the Lord and set me down in the middle of the valley; it was full of bones" (vv. 1). Ezekiel walked back and forth, surveying what was in front of him. What he saw were bones too numerous to count.

God then asked Ezekiel the simple but potent question, "Son of man, can these bones live?" (vv. 3)

What God really meant was, do you have eyes to see the life potential in the midst of death and destruction? Can you look at what is evidently lifeless and envision resurrection?

It's a question he still asks us today as we wrestle and wait. Despite the dry bones we may see—the hopeless situations, unrepaired relationships, or stagnant dreams—can we believe for God to bring forth life even still?

Ezekiel, seemingly a wise man, replied that only God knew if the bones would live and rise again. God then commanded Ezekiel to prophesy words infused with power over the bones, declaring breath to enter and restoration to come. God promised tendons and flesh would appear again, signs of future life and purpose.

Ezekiel obeyed and proclaimed the *wills* of God: "I *will* make breath enter you, and you *will* come to life. I *will* attach tendons to you and make flesh come upon you and cover you with skin; I *will* put breath in you, and you *will* come to life. Then you *will* know that I am the Lord" (vv. 5-6 NIV, emphasis mine). Ezekiel voiced God's promises over the valley of dry bones. Though he saw death, life was coming.

Ezekiel did exactly as God directed him to do and witnessed as bones too numerous to count began to rattle and connect together. Imagine the sheer amazement, and terror, as Ezekiel watched what was happening. As much as we believe God can use us and that our voices have power, there's also the question of *if* we will see anything take place with our own eyes. But Ezekiel, in the middle of this valley of dry bones, spoke out what God said. And as he did, bones moved. The rattling began. What was dry and broken revived and repaired to wholeness. Bones connected to bones, tendons formed, and skin appeared.

In a valley of death Ezekiel beheld God restore by doing what God asked him to do—to prophesy life.

Yet even with all that had occurred, breath was still missing. And there is no life without breath. There is no life for our bodies or our spirits without the inhale and exhale.

God again instructed Ezekiel to prophesy. This time, though, his words weren't directed to the physical bones but to the invisible breath. Ezekiel did as God commanded and called for the all-encompassing breath to "come from the four winds...and breathe on these slain, that they may live" (vv. 9).

At first Ezekiel prophesied to the bones, restoring form and structure to what he physically saw in front of him. By his words the bones were fused together with flesh and tendons. Now God directed Ezekiel to prophesy to what he could not see, the breath of God and the invisible wind. God intended to revive the seen by a release of the unseen.

Ezekiel prophesied into the bones and by God's words spoken through his mouth, "breath came into them, and they lived and stood on their feet, an exceedingly great army" (vv. 10). Not only did Ezekiel speak and life happened, but a whole army stood to its feet. One man, called by God to prophesy, influenced an entire reality by simply releasing the words God commanded.

There will be countless seasons in your life when you will stand upon seemingly barren land as you wait. When you will look around and easily bear witness to what has not happened. When you will be flooded with reminders of how others are receiving what you hope for while you remain overwhelmed by lack, despair, or delay. And like Ezekiel, you will be asked if you can see life potential in the middle of the dry valley. Can you carry vision beyond your circumstances?

It takes no faith to identify what is literally right in front of you or what isn't going as planned. And it is no easy task to believe for what you cannot taste or touch. Faith requires you to lift your sights higher than the storm or the mountain for what remains possible. So the question is, Can you see?

❧

Hebrews 11 recounts the great heroes of the past who believed in God despite impossible situations. Among them were Noah, Abraham, and Sarah, those who held vision greater than what their circumstances evidenced. The author described the faith they carried and then wrote, "These all died in faith, not having received the things promised, but having seen them and greeted them from afar, and having acknowledged that they were strangers and exiles on the earth" (vv. 13).

What did these people have in common? They died in faith. They didn't receive all that was promised to them. But also, they saw the potential. From afar, though they didn't fully experience it, they perceived what could be in the middle of what was. They were surrounded by pressure yet they envisioned promise.

This is faith in action. This is what God sought in Ezekiel and what he searches for in us. No matter what we see today, even if it screams of impossibilities, can we remain confident for how God will affect our reality? And with bold faith, can we declare life, blessing, and hope into what is absent, barren, or seemingly impossible?

The circumstances of our lives aren't meant to determine or define the words we speak. Instead, with courage and wonder, even in pain and disappointment, we are to release words that proclaim God is faithful to fulfill what he promises to do.

Being prophetic people who see and speak life is essential to the journey, especially when waiting. We must tune our ears to hear God's whisper to us and then we must open our mouths to release those words into our season. Why? Because words of power transform our days.

Practically, this may look like you recognizing the lack of deep friendships in your life and then praying words of expectancy that God will surround you with community. Or thanking God for how he is shifting your season through a breakup or job loss, believing for the opportunities he is giving to you. Or receiving that rejection for graduate school, a book deal, or an ideal job fit and still declaring God is moving, connecting, and propelling you.

Living prophetically means upgrading how you perceive and engage your season. It means anticipating that God is always doing "immeasurably more than all we ask or imagine" (Ephesians 3:20 NIV). So you release words, take risks, and approach today by connecting to what God is saying and how he is moving.

❧

The vision of Ezekiel among the dry bones contains specific meaning within the context of the time and it also speaks to us today. The

Bible is the inspiration of God so what God breathed on those generations long ago still holds his power as we read it. So what can we pull from Ezekiel's encounter with God in the valley of dry bones?

First, as God's children we can trust that we hear his voice. He is the God of connection and covenant. He always has been and will be. So we can hear God's promises and truths. We can discern his direction and guidance.

All throughout history God communicated to his people in crucial moments. He spoke to Abraham and called him to leave all he knew to go where God was sending him so that future generations would be blessed through him (Genesis 12:1-3). He spoke to Moses as a friend (Exodus 33:11) and gave him the commandments on Mount Sinai to guide his people to their promise. He instructed his prophets, including Isaiah, Jeremiah and Ezekiel. In the New Testament, God continued to communicate. He spoke through his messenger to Mary about the child she would conceive (Luke 1:30-33) and to Jesus when he was baptized in the Jordan River (Matthew 3:17). And, of course, God interrupted Paul's entire plan and purpose when he spoke to him on his way to Damascus (Acts 9:4).

God's nature is one of communication and relationship, and he hasn't stopped speaking today. Because of all Jesus did, an intimate relationship with God is now accessible to all people (and not just a select few).

Not only is God talking to us, but we can tune in to hear his voice and receive direction from him. Jesus made it clear that for those who are God's sheep with him as their shepherd, they both hear and know his voice (John 10:4). We may think God's voice has to be audible, forceful, or follow such words as "Thus saith." But in actuality, it is often a quiet whisper spoken to our hearts in such a way that no other ears but our own hear his words for us. Somehow,

150

far beyond our rationale or ability to articulate by logical words, we sense when God is saying something to us. There's simplicity and mystery to it. We can't explain it, but we know it.

Just as Ezekiel heard God speak to him, God is still communicating to us today. So the question for us is, What is he saying?

❧

Secondly, Ezekiel 37 emphasizes that our voices are able to release life into the world. I remember when I first became aware that my words had the ability to impact my environment. Like I mentioned in chapter 1, I struggled with my voice for most of high school and college. But then I began learning about the power of my voice and how there's always an opportunity to declare words of life. I started to grasp the truth that "death and life are in the power of the tongue" (Proverbs 18:21). Or as *The Message* writes it, "Words kill, words give life; they're poison or fruit—you choose."

When we lean in to hear what God is saying, we are then offered the opportunity to impart his words into the environment around us. Ezekiel saw death in front of him and, by what he heard God command, he prophesied words that changed the valley of dry bones into a living army. Our voices proclaiming God's words extend this same transformation to the world. We can release power into what is barren and dry. We can witness our words resurrect life.

Sometimes we think being prophetic requires some ministerial office or dramatic moment of calling by God. But we've all been commissioned by him to prophesy with purpose and power. Paul instructed the early church that "you may all prophesy in turn" (1 Corinthians 14:31 NIV). He wasn't claiming that everyone is called to be a prophet and appointed to the prophetic office of ministry.

He was saying that all of us are empowered by the Holy Spirit in us to survey and transform our present reality by aligning our words with what God is saying.

In fact, Paul urged followers of Jesus to "earnestly desire the spiritual gifts, especially that you may prophesy" (vv. 1). He specifically wanted people to receive this gift so they would be a voice of life and blessing to the world. And he instructed them to prophesy for people's "strengthening, encouraging and comfort" (vv. 3 NIV). These words are meant to edify others by revealing what God is saying. While every encouraging word is not prophetic, every prophetic word is encouraging. Every comforting word may not be what God is saying right now, but the words he asks us to voice will extend his comfort.

First we lean in and listen. Then we speak and release God's breath. All with the intention to influence, affect, and resurrect the people, places, and problems where God is moving. So proclaiming that God is still active and present. Nothing is too far gone or lost for him to work through.

Declaring words that reflect God's voice can look a variety of ways in everyday life. For me, one of the first things that happens in the morning is leading Eloise through declarations on our way to her preschool. It's such a simple habit that regularly reminds her of what God says about her. By now it's so ingrained in our drive that she makes sure we do them even if I forget. Sometimes she leads them, sometimes I do. But each day she proclaims words of purpose. She declares over herself that she is full of courage, joy, and kindness. She proclaims that God loves her, has a plan for her, and delights in her. She reminds herself who and whose she is before ever stepping foot into her school.

This practice is also one of the best weapons for discouragement or insecurity, especially on those "off" days when I wake up in a rough spot. I don't let myself dwell there. Instead, I walk to the bathroom, look in the mirror, and remind myself of who I am. Or I begin to thank God for everything he is doing and has done. Or I take a deep breath, quiet down, and listen to what God is saying to me in the middle of my heaviness.

Prophesying can be as simple as calling a friend because of an internal prompting and reminding her of what God is saying over her. Or deciding you will carry a faith-filled vision for how God is moving at work or school or within your home, determining to believe that God is doing more than you presently know. Or considering the people who irritate or offend you the most in your day and asking God who he has made them to be, shifting your conversations to focus on their value and purpose in God's kingdom.

⸕

Finally, Ezekiel 37 charges us to expect God to transform. Repeatedly God instructs Ezekiel on what to say, specifically what he will do. *I will cause life to happen. I will have breath enter. I will raise them to life. I will, I will, I will,* God promised.

When we hear God speak, we are then invited to anticipate how he will change what is before us. As the author of Hebrews writes, "By faith we understand that the universe was created by the word of God, so that what is seen was not made out of things that are visible" (Hebrews 11:3). God's words create. And now his words dwell in us because Christ, the Word of God, lives in us.

So we are called to prophesy into what is currently unseen and believe that what is in heaven will invade what is on earth. To expect that what we cannot see will reshape and restore what we can see. To trust firmly that God longs to release his kingdom on earth and that when we speak his words, they shape both the present and the future.

No matter your current situation or season of waiting, God is commissioning you to be a prophetic voice of love, honor, and blessing in the world. Why? So that what you see in the natural is supernaturally changed by what you cannot see, God's Spirit living and moving through you.

❧

While there have been many seasons when I have witnessed God do the impossible, there have been others when my eyes were clouded and I was unable to identify potential possibilities. So my voice went quiet.

When we lose our vision for what could be, we typically begin to feel stuck, stricken with fear, or just plain lost. And when we are there, the best thing to do is to inspire our voice again.

What I've learned in seasons of drought is to whisper to myself who I am, what I am promised, and who I am resting under. It matters less what the world around me is encouraging and so much more what God is whispering.

We have the opportunity every day to speak over ourselves words that stir fresh hope, focus, and love into our lives. We can remind ourselves of our confidence, purpose, and passion. Then we can trust those words, rest into them, and go about our days secure that we are exactly who God says we are.

Your voice matters, over your own life and especially in your waiting. Aligned with God's promises and truth, your words carry the potential to alter your mindset, infiltrate your environment with heavenly peace, strengthen your marriage, and pray purpose into your children's futures. They remind you that God is not done, you have not missed it, and you are not behind. They declare that God's promise for you is still alive and active. His plans are still unfolding. And that you will taste and see the goodness of God in the land of the living.

When you speak words filled with hope and life, you remind yourself of what God has promised. Those words secure you to his presence and his movement. They anchor you to his power and his purpose. So as you remember again to live this day by inhaling and exhaling God with you, may you release words of expectancy over what has yet to come. For he is the God who resurrects dry bones into living armies.

CHAPTER TWELVE

HISTORY WILL DETERMINE

Mark and I were newly engaged and eager to begin wedding planning. We kept asking our friends where we should register and learned that in the wedding world, at that time, Bed Bath & Beyond was top of the list. Not knowing what we were doing or having a clue what we needed, we went to check out things on a late Sunday afternoon.

Being handed that nifty gun to scan whatever we wanted was fun in theory, until it came time to actually make decisions. We had absolutely no idea what knives we wanted, let alone bakeware, cookware, or kitchenware. We became overwhelmed by all the options. So with a simple nod we dropped the gun back on the wedding registry desk and left for our favorite restaurant.

We took the more scenic route to dinner, one of those long-stretching country roads with wide lanes and not much to look at but green fields and trees. We were laughing our way through the debacle of the last hour when we came to a red light. The skies were just about to open up with its next spring downpour. Mark was driving and he slowed to a stop as we watched the cars in the left lane turn into the new gas station.

All of a sudden one of those cars got sideswiped by another car and instantly burst into flames. In total disbelief we watched as a man and woman grabbed their young child. They ran from their burning car to safety underneath the awning of the gas pumps.

The minute Mark and I witnessed this whole tragedy unfold, we had a serious choice to make and something in us knew what we were being asked to do.

Cars around us quickly sped off to their intended destinations as the light turned green again, I'm sure sympathetic to what they had witnessed but not driven to do anything about it. For all the stories I've shared about God's power moving all over the world, this was one situation that put to the test who we would be in the middle of an urgent need. Mark and I knew our presence wasn't necessary since plenty of ambulances and policemen would be showing up imminently to help. While this family would be physically taken care of, what if we were being asked to offer something unique to them?

Somehow I was aware that this choice was going to become a defining moment, putting into action what I say I want my life to be about—like God using me in unexpected and spontaneous ways, being someone who is more focused on ushering in his kingdom than accomplishing my plans, and releasing into others what God has graciously poured into my life.

With pounding hearts and sweaty hands, we pulled our car into the mayhem at the gas station and walked up to the couple. They were standing close together under the side of an adjacent building to shield themselves from the rain that was now pouring down. The husband's arm was wrapped tightly around his wife, who held their eighteen-month-old son. A policeman was with them and had just finished taking their statement.

We greeted them with as much compassion and care as we could express, then explained that we had seen the accident happen and couldn't leave without coming over to them. They were visibly shaken up. The husband gave us one of those half smiles in an attempt to appease our desire to help and then turned his gaze on his family.

Neither of us were deterred by his lack of interest in a conversation, so I asked them, "Can we pray over your family? We know there's a reason we were here when the accident took place. We'd love to ask God to move through all that's happened today."

They replied with kind but quiet yeses, and we all huddled together—Mark, me, this shocked family, and the lone policeman.

Noises and voices were stirring all around us, as were the sounds of beeping tow trucks and distant sirens. Mark and I shared simple words of blessing, peace, and comfort over this family. We prayed that God would move in mighty ways and invade this place with his presence.

"In Jesus' name, Amen." We looked up to see the policeman rather thankful that the prayer was over, though the family already appeared a bit more calm.

"How are you feeling?" I asked. "Not only do we believe that God wants to pour out his peace on you but also any healing needed. Did any of you get hurt in the accident?"

"My ankle is all busted," the husband replied.

"This may sound crazy, but can we lay hands on your ankle and pray for God's healing power to come and realign whatever is out of sorts? We're confident God is here with us in all of this."

The husband agreed, so Mark and I bent down on our knees and placed our hands on his ankle. We prayed that all pain would go and healing would come. After we were done we asked him to move it around and he said it was still hurting. Once more we knelt down on the ground, laid hands on his ankle, and believed for God to touch him.

Saying he felt noticeable relief, Mark asked one final question. "What else can we do for you? What do you need? We're here and available."

This was the first time the wife spoke up. "It was our wedding day yesterday," she said as tears streamed down both their faces. "We were on our way to our honeymoon this afternoon when this all happened. All our gifts were in the trunk..." She couldn't keep talking. The reality of what was lost overcame her with sadness.

Picking up where she left off, the husband said, "We don't have anything for our son. All his stuff for our trip was in that car."

Overflowing with love for this family, we were ready to care for them exactly where they were. I exclaimed, "No problem! There's a Walmart just a mile down the road. Tell us what you need and we'll get it for you." Mark jotted down things like a car seat, bottles, diapers, and wipes. Totally doable, I thought, and off we went.

Mark and I traded the overwhelming options of Bed Bath & Beyond for the unending ones of baby world. We walked into Walmart, found the appropriate aisle, and had an eye-opening experience. I used my phone to search for answers to questions like, "How much does an 18-month-old weigh?" or "What kind of bottle does a toddler typically use?" We tried calling our only friends who had a child at the time in hopes they could offer us some direction, but they didn't pick up. So we filled our cart with our best guesses and drove back to the family.

By then their friend had arrived. We brought the car seat over to the minivan to be installed and then unloaded the rest of the bags in the trunk. Tired, exhausted, and ready to get out of there, the husband and wife looked at us with eyes of gratitude. We hugged them, spoke words of increased blessings over them, and told them it was our joy to be able to help.

By the time they got in their car to drive away, the whole atmosphere had changed. Instead of being a place of chaos, confusion, and loss, it was a realm in which all of us were reminded through simple acts of love that God is with us in the middle of the mess. As we drove away I kept thinking how I couldn't imagine missing the opportunity that afternoon to partner with God in revealing his presence to his people in need.

I caught hold of an understanding that day that if I keep my ears open, lean into God's voice, and follow where he leads, I will be given countless opportunities to influence what is taking place around me. It has little to do with where I am standing or what my present reality looks like. Though I may personally be waiting on something specific, I am still empowered by God to impact my environment.

And that's the powerful truth that combats the lies we talked about earlier, the ones that whisper to us that we are forgotten, disqualified, or lacking. The ones that say we don't have anything to offer until we receive whatever it is we are hoping for. Rather, the opportunity is that we can turn our eyes from what is happening *to* us and focus on how to participate in where God is moving *around* us.

⁂

When I was leading a weekly women's Bible study a few years ago, I experienced a powerful revelation that changed how I understand my responsibility for showing up and living my present season.

The very first week of our study was on chapter 1 of the book of Mark. It was about the dawn of the new day when Jesus came, the long awaited and hoped for manifestation of God's love and commitment. Early on in the chapter it becomes clear that God had commissioned John the Baptist to prepare the way for Jesus. While John was baptizing in the Jordan River, Jesus came to him and asked John to baptize him too. As Jesus emerged out of the water, he "saw the heavens being torn open and the Spirit descending on him like a dove" (vv. 10). God ripped open the skies and his Spirit came down.

One of the powerful elements of this baptismal moment is that centuries prior God's people had cried out for him to do that exact thing. They prayed that God "would rend the heavens and come down, that the mountains might quake at your presence" (Isaiah 64:1). Woven throughout the Old Testament was the yearning of God's people for the fulfillment of the promised Messiah. They hoped for God to restore his relationship with them and bestow his blessings upon them.

Yet like it often is for us and certainly was for them, waiting ushered in their breakthrough. What preceded Jesus' arrival was four hundred years of quiet by God. During this season, numerous and intense troubles broke out among the people. Persecution was rampant, idolatry was widespread, and revolts and battles were common. Even so, God's stillness continued until Jesus was born. His coming loudly declared that it was a new day and a new era for God's people. Despite all their messes and mistakes, God responded to their prayers and followed through on his promise for the Messiah. Emmanuel arrived.

God then tore open the heavens at Jesus' baptism when he emerged from the water. He did exactly what the people had implored him to do. God heard their prayers and fulfilled their waiting that spanned generations. And as the sky was ripped, Jesus experienced a powerful moment of commissioning. The Spirit came down and rested upon him like a dove, and the Father proclaimed him to be his Son. Jesus then launched into the desert where he was tempted for forty days. He returned in the power of the Spirit, equipped to accomplish what God was calling him to do.

As I read through the account of Jesus' baptism in preparation for my Bible study, I was struck with the realization that the heavens are *still open*. They were violently ripped apart and never sewn up again. What God did in that moment remains our reality today. We have total access to God and his presence with us because of the open heaven above us. There is no limit or restriction to what God can do. The Spirit is in us, resting on us, and moving all around us. No longer must we pray for access to God. We have it. Instead, we pray for God to increase our awareness of all he has accomplished for us and given to us.

And the mind-blowing truth is that through Jesus, the power that raised him from the dead *now lives in us* (Romans 8:11). The Spirit that resides in us through Christ *is* the resurrection power of God. Power that repairs, restores, and revives. Power that offers the people and places around us an encounter with God that leaves them never the same again. No matter our circumstance or struggle, where we stand or where we go, we can press into God's presence with us and release his life-transforming power from us. Even as we wait and wrestle and hope.

The prayer Jesus taught his disciples begins with the words, "Our Father in heaven, hallowed be your name. Your kingdom come, your will be done, on earth as it is in heaven" (Matthew 6:9-13). Jesus equipped his followers to approach God as Father and expectantly declare God's will to be done. He also revealed the purpose of God's access, presence, and power. Specifically, that what we see reflects the reality of what we cannot see. For earth to bear the image of heaven in an ever-increasing measure.

This is the mandate for our days and our seasons. We show up where we are and engage with God there. Not solely for the moment but for the ongoing and unfolding encounter that transforms our world to be as heaven above. We access God to receive all he has done and given to us, so that what flows from our lives restores the world around us.

So practically what does this look like? At times this looks like your willingness to say yes when the unexpected interrupts your day, whether it is a financial need you can meet, a person you can serve, or a prayer you can speak in faith. Or it may look like increasing your awareness of God's activity. To walk into a store consciously identifying where there is an earnest cry for fresh hope or an opportunity to be a voice of life to someone who feels lost. Other times it looks like you tapping into God's heart of love for others, even people you struggle with, and consider how you can reveal God's reality to them. Ultimately, it looks like where there is lack, you offer provision. Where there is despair, you impart hope. Where there is fear, you release love.

Why? So that what is in you may be given to those around you. And God's presence is the greatest offering you have as you show up to your day and live out your season. This is the gift. This is the opportunity and the commission, even and especially in your waiting.

❦

This book has explored how we encounter God in the middle of our waiting seasons. But it's so important to understand that we experience him so that we extend encounters to those around us. What changes the atmosphere is the invitation to another person that in their distress or mess, they can meet the real and active God.

Not long ago Eloise and I visited our neighborhood Target to pick up some groceries. I probably showed up at this Target at least twice a week because, well, it's Target. Eloise was at the age when she thought sitting in the top of the grocery cart was the best thing ever. So I put her in and turned to go on our normal route around the store. Suddenly, my eyes locked on a young woman nearby who was limping in the front entrance. Her brown hair was thrown up in a messy bun and she was wearing athletic clothes. Yet what I really noticed was her left foot, which was in a perpetual high-heeled position with an ace bandage wrapped around it. All it took was one glance to know this woman was in a lot of pain.

I turned back to Eloise not thinking much of it until I felt that deep inner pull from God, the one that suggests that this isn't a situation to take note of but one to go participate in. God immediately reminded me of when I watched him heal Fissy in South Africa. Then I heard him whisper to me, "What will you do with what you see right now?"

There was no mistaking the moment. God was inviting me to consider how I might partner with him in changing the environment while in one of the most ordinary places, my local Target. I'd love to say that I instantly and boldly approached her about praying over her foot, but truthfully I fought this nudge the entire shopping trip. I desperately wanted to step into what God was doing, but I also felt unsure and awkward.

Around the Target Eloise and I went. Outside everything looked normal, but inwardly I was wrestling between God's nudging and my own discomfort and trepidation. I held an intense conversation with God as we walked the aisles. I was trying all I could to assuage this urge within me to take part in what he might want to do through me. He was, in turn, reminding me that whether I stepped into this or not didn't determine his love for me but could showcase his love through me.

What added comedy to the whole situation was that I ran into this woman at least six times as we went around the store. Time and again I would turn down the clothing, food, shoes, or toiletries aisle and there she was. Every single time. Finally I got to the point where

I had battled long enough and surrendered myself to what God was doing. I let it be known to him that my deepest longing was to participate where he was moving no matter the fool I might make of myself. "Okay," I resolved, "when I see her next I will go up to her and ask her if I can pray for her. This time I'll do it."

Sure enough, there she was standing in the vegetable aisle. I strolled up to her and said, "Excuse me. Hi. I'm sorry to bother you, but I haven't been able to stop noticing that you're limping through here. I actually have witnessed God heal people in the past of ankle problems and was hoping I could quickly pray for you too?"

Kind of stunned by my question, she let out an exhale. "I literally have tried everything and I just came back from getting X-rays today. I've done acupuncture, physical therapy, everything. I don't know what's wrong with my foot."

"Well, would it be okay if I prayed right here and asked God to heal you?"

She agreed, I hunched over, and touched her ankle with my hand believing that God would impart power, health, and alignment back into her foot in Jesus' name. When I was done praying, I stood back up and smiled at her. Though she didn't instantly say everything was better, I didn't push her on it either. I sensed there was more God was doing than I was aware of in that moment of me praying.

I noticed when looking in her eyes that she carried a fresh peace and presence to her. I was sure God had met her in the middle of her pain. Though I've yet to see her again, I still expect I may as God often reconnects us to moments and people like this. One act of saying yes to the opportunity God had before me and we were both overwhelmed by his presence within our ordinary realms.

While I drove home that day from this encounter, I realized God had moved in more ways that I initially recognized when my world collided with this woman's. First, to be able to release God's heart and ask for his Spirit to come in the middle of Target is a powerful invitation. The whole exchange reminded me on that mundane Thursday that changing the atmosphere isn't only for the great giants of the faith or in extreme settings. It's also for times like a weekly grocery run. Because there, in one of my most frequented places, God's kingdom is meant to be released.

Second, I watched as this woman's environment shifted. She walked away knowing that God had seen her. He cared for what she was wrestling through as she was stuck in her waiting for answers and healing. He touched and encountered her, right there amid her pain.

And finally, I had my own revival. I ditched the lie that tries to convince me I'm "just a mom." Though it may be something completely different for you, there are subtle words whispered that discredit us and seize opportunities from us. God didn't disqualify me; he commissioned me. He was sending me out in the middle of my normal routine to extend encounters to others in the mess of their waiting. Tears streamed down my face as I drove home that day. I prayed out loud to God, "*This* is what I want to give my life to. That revival would come through my family despite any of our fears and worries. I pray revival is always in us so it can flow through us."

What I love about what took place at Target is that it was such an ordinary setting and I am such a normal person with all kinds of barriers to work through. Yet, even with my fears swirling, an extraordinary God decided to invade the mundane and affect the environment. There wasn't anything spectacular about this day, this place, or me in the slightest. So don't believe the thought that you need to "get it together" before you try your hand at listening and following God's lead wherever it takes you. It doesn't matter how scared you may be or ill-equipped you may feel. How I pray you go anyway. Fear, weakness, and worry can be companions if they must. Because even more powerful is that fire in your belly that wants to change the world far more than sit on the sidelines.

You may be waiting on huge things today from God and still there are opportunities in your typical day to reflect his kingdom come. That is the beautiful gift. There are always invitations to lean into God's nudging and determine that despite all that may be holding you back, today you're going for it.

Vegetable aisle and trembling hands and all.

※

After ten semesters studying Greek and Hebrew in seminary, my last paper of my final language course required me to pick a passage from Isaiah and produce over forty pages of insights. Definitely not for the faint of heart. Instantly, though, I knew my passage:

"Arise, shine, for your light has come, and the glory of the Lord has risen upon you. For behold, darkness shall cover the earth, and thick darkness the peoples; but the Lord will arise upon you, and his glory will be seen upon you. And nations shall come to your light, and kings to the brightness of your rising." (Isaiah 60:1-3)

The context of it has to do with God fulfilling his promises to his people who were exiled at the time. They wondered if he would still remember them despite their sins and errors. God's pronouncement here was for them to arise because of all he had done and still planned to do. God hadn't forgotten. He would accomplish what he had declared.

I've always been drawn to this passage. Partly because it carries such promise with it and also because there is a charge to it. What excites me is the connection between the promise and the charge. God's people are to arise *in order that* what they are waiting on can manifest to its fullest. Arise and shine, God commanded. Why? So he too would rise and shine his glory. Woven deeply here was the mandate for his people to get moving in their waiting, which stirred God to bring forth the fulfillment of his promises. In order for nations to come to the light and kings to the brightness, God's people had to arise. In their waiting God clearly commanded his people to action and not passivity.

Don't waste time as you wait, he essentially said, but get up and stand tall exactly where you are. Reflect the reality of my presence to the world around, because of what I have done for you and all you anticipate I will do through you.

God is not done. So arise and shine even when the season feels never-ending and the outward circumstances have yet to change. Because as we get up and radiate God's glory, God also arises and shines brightly upon us. The result is a beautiful partnership of God and his people instep with one another, trusting each other. Both rising and radiating to love and transform the world, together.

No matter where you are today, I believe God longs to use you right here. Not to wait until things change to step into all you are meant to do or be. But to be present and alert in this waiting season, on this very day.

Delaying to become who he's called you to be or to do what he's asking you to do until he moves you elsewhere is the postponement of your calling and identity. All around you are people wondering how in the world they will ever see the thing they desperately hope to receive. Instead of passively waiting and wasting time, resources, and opportunities until you advance from your season, may you walk boldly in the middle of what God is doing here.

My prayer for you is that you may rest deeply into exactly where you stand, settled that God has you where you are meant to be. But also that you may close this book with a fire burning in you that ignites your eyes to see, ears to hear, voice to speak, and courage to give to the world. One person and one opportunity at a time. Not by your determination alone but by the power of God realized and released from you—even with your weaknesses as companions of grace on the journey.

⁂

When Mark and I spent our summer in Mozambique as newlyweds we heard words one day that I have never been able to shake. A woman was speaking to us as we sat on the hard concrete ground for hours on end. It was hot, my back was aching, and there was mild chaos all around with children running and yelling. But still I did my best to keep listening to what she was sharing.

She was emotional through most of what she spoke, with tears continuously streaming down her face and sniffles running throughout her hour-long talk. Her narrative was one of trust and hope along an unexpected journey that included loss, like her mom dying, and personal victory, like getting to preach in front of her greatest heroes. Then she closed with words I will never forget. They're not from her own life but were part of a vision her pastor had shared with her and their church body. Though they are from his personal experience with God, they carry a divine charge with them for those of us who wait, who hope, and who long to see the world around us reflect the fullness of God within us.

As she finished her talk, she concluded with these words: "And history will determine if you believed him."

What she meant is that history will tell if we stood up and stood firm in the middle of our waiting to partner with God in what he was doing around us. History will testify if we believed God to be faithful to all he said he would do when we couldn't see any of it. History will determine if we were willing to wait in the middle of today for God's release, goodness, and fulfillment ahead. Our words won't secure such things nor will our deepest desires. Our history will reveal if we believed, trusted, and fiercely hoped. We will look back one day on all we did or didn't do and tell of how our resting reflected our waiting on God and how our moving was by his leading.

It's the history of *his story in us* that will declare whether we chose to trust God as we waited and whether we chose to make our waiting count for so much more than ourselves. How I pray we do. I carry those words with me as a constant reminder. It's my history that will speak the best story of how I engaged with God in my waiting and extended encounters to the world around me.

Our history, that's what will proclaim it.

So may we be those who hold within us both the anticipation of God fulfilling his promises in the days ahead as well as such an awareness of him commissioning us in the waiting of today.

To arise and shine.
To get up and reflect.
To stand and wait

SELAH

I was tempted to close out this whole journey making the last word of the final chapter, *selah*.

If you've done much reading through the book of Psalms then you've definitely come across this word time and again. Yet if you were to look it up in a Hebrew dictionary to find out its meaning, you may be surprised to learn that it's often defined in obscure, indefinite terms. "It means something like" or "whose meaning is uncertain," as the definition typically reads.

Since psalms were sung to music and melodies, those who put together the Hebrew Bible interjected this word throughout certain songs at specific moments for one purpose.

To pause.

They would sing and proclaim, declare and pronounce. Then stop. Rest. Consider what has been said, what God has done, and what is still promised ahead.

Selah.

There aren't perfect English words to capture all it means because it's really less about a definition and so much more about a sense, a release, a rest. Because no matter how much clarity or revelation we may achieve about our seasons and God's intentions for them, there's still the mystery. Always the unknown.

What an unbelievable gift it is to have mystery in the waiting. It keeps us from being so foolish to think we have it all figured out or know all the steps from here on out. It's what draws us close, leaned in and listening.

Waiting has never been about the destination or the arrival at some point down the road. It's always been about the pilgrimage, the journey of awakening and maturing. And the process we undertake carries the pause between where we are and where we will be, who we are and who we will become.

So we, too, must stop and take a breath along the way, resting and pausing at key moments and impasses in order to receive and remember...

Who we are and who God is.

What he calls us to do and how he calls us to rest.

How he's hidden and how he's seen.

What he's whispering and what he's showing.

In many ways this book has been my personal selah, an interjection between verses of a greater song to breathe and reflect. For years I have found myself waiting, hoping, and not seeing. Some days I naively think it's coming to a close, but in reality I know that the waiting will always, graciously, be there. It is my ever-present invitation to trust when I do not know and go where I cannot see.

So the words of this book are my pause.

You may think that means that my outward circumstances have quieted down enough to afford me the opportunity to write in peaceful reflection. In comical reality, this current season is hot with movement, transitions, and opportunities to become caught up in the destination over the journey.

As I pen these final words, I'm halfway through my third pregnancy while mothering a one-year-old and three-year-old, both who I spend my days merely trying to keep up with. It mostly looks like me attempting to herd cats, only with a giant belly attached to me. My husband recently made the biggest career move of his life, which transitioned us to a new city where we are now in the process of making our home. Each day I wake up to the joys of so many gifts in life and also the delay of dreams that I have not yet tasted or seen.

Though this book is my selah, it has been offered up in the middle of both my chaos and my waiting.

I used to worry about showcasing an arrived woman to the world, thinking that if I masqueraded as her then maybe one day I would become her. But today I am less prone to do that because I am finding that my weaknesses are in fact my gifts. When I am in the middle of the process—uncertain, dependent, and learning as I go—I am at my best to the world around me. How ironic a thought, simultaneously terrifying and relieving to accept.

And in my waiting, always my waiting, how I have encountered God. Over and over, season and years past, each and every time I have found myself here, I have met him. He has been faithful. And the journey has been far more my teacher than any arrival has ever been.

As I close out this book, I pray that you and I are both able to embrace and celebrate the untranslatable moments just as much as the planned and understood ones.

May we welcome mystery into the seasons of our lives.

May we hear and respond to the call to pause and reflect more often than we yield to the urge to strive and fix.

May we breathe deeply, lift our eyes, and live in the powerful moment of whatever is right now.

And may we confidently anticipate that good things come in the land of the living and in the middle of our waiting.

No matter what we long for, no matter what we wait upon, no matter how long it has been or will be ahead, today is the invitation to encounter God just as we are and with all that he is. Today is our gift, and today is our offering.

So my friend, selah.

CHOICES IN THE WAITING

Determining what to do in the middle of our waiting can be a complex thing to figure out. Do we rest in our waiting? Get moving? Do something, don't do something, try something new? We've already talked about discernment, which speaks to our ability to know whether or not we make a move. But what about what we *do* as we wait? Like we've discussed throughout the book, in seasons of waiting we're gifted with choice. We're not passive pawns aimlessly wandering through time until the season changes. That's both boring and ineffective.

Instead, we're called to be alert and active participants exactly where we find ourselves in order that our waiting carries breakthrough. Isn't that what we're all longing for as we continue to wait where we stand? Breakthrough. The entrance of something new that invades our world. And though breakthrough rarely comes quickly, it certainly arrives suddenly.

So how do we get moving toward breakthrough as we stand in the middle of our waiting? And what practical actions can we take to be fully engaged in what God is doing?

Those are the questions this appendix seeks to answer because we are never void of choices as we wait. And using the discernment gifted to us, we can make intentional and purposeful ones that enable us to transform our surroundings.

Below you'll find thoughts and stories on a few of the options present in the waiting. While the list isn't exhaustive, it touches on distinct pathways to consider as you decide how God is leading you.

Because the choices you make as you wait reflect your active partnership with God.

❧

THE CHOICE TO DO

Four years ago I set out to write my first book. I didn't have a clue how to do this so I enlisted the help of a friend. At the time she was in the editing process for her forthcoming book and was full of knowledge. The first thing I learned from her was that I needed a book proposal. No problem, I thought. One quick search led me to Michael Hyatt's "Write a Winning Book Proposal" and I immediately bought it.

Over the next weeks and months I pieced together the proposal. It contained every bit of information about my topic that a publisher wants to know, from a compelling summary and thorough market analysis to the initial chapter of my incomplete manuscript.

I felt proud of that book proposal. I spent a lot of time on it, received so much help from others, and was eager to get it into the right hands. Soon after, I was connected with a few Christian publishing houses. According to the guidelines of one of them, they were unwilling to read proposals from authors without an agent. Yet somehow an unexpected door opened that allowed my proposal to arrive into those influential hands.

This was amazing news for me, to which I was sure even better news would follow.

It didn't take long for emails to start showing up in my inbox. They all carried a similar message. This was well done, they applauded, but we're not interested. The news crushed me. The fact I was certain it was a season of breakthrough made it extra hard for me to swallow the rejection.

I quickly translated the news of not wanting to publish my book to mean I was a poor writer who shouldn't pursue writing one. I didn't know how to keep moving forward on something those official voices stamped as not good enough.

So I put my book proposal aside and willed myself to forget about it. It sat there for years before I began to hear God's whisper remind me of my dream to write a book. Something was different this time, though, because I didn't feel him leading me to craft another proposal or pitch the one I had to more publishing houses. Instead, I sensed him inviting me to actually write a book.

It was a total shift for me. Rather than waiting for an outside voice to grant me permission to pursue this dream, God was the one asking me to write and release what was already within me. This was about stewardship and giving away what God had deposited. Writing a book was about me changing my source of permission from external voices to his internal whisper.

So day by day and word by word I wrote that book. I finished it, edited it, and had others review it—and now you're reading it.

I stopped waiting for validation from a publisher. I stopped waiting for someone to discover me or applaud my writing before I actually did the work. Rather, I wrote the book. I took back permission from others and launched forward by God's leading smack in the middle of my waiting.

Sometimes breakthrough comes by God's instant change when he suddenly moves on our behalf. Other times the breakthrough arrives by our choice to get going before the promise manifests. That's when the waiting requires our doing long before we see, taste, or touch what we hope for ahead.

This typically happens when our waiting has more to do with our fears than God's inactivity. We can, at times, hide under the encompassing umbrella of "waiting" because we're scared of what a promise in motion would actually require of us. As frustrating as the pause or delay can be, it can become a safe harbor for us compared to the faith demanded to move out.

After another day with no forward traction, we may scream to God a resounding, "What are you waiting for?" Our cry comes with a footnote such as, "If you would only move or open that door, then I could step into the things promised for my life."

We can't be sure what kind of answer will be given. But at times, we will hear those words boomerang back to us asking in reply, "What are *you* waiting for?"

Because sometimes our waiting requires our doing, before our seeing, in order to move us into our promise.

When the Israelites were in the wilderness and preparing to cross over into the Promised Land after forty years of waiting, Moses charged them with these words: "Cross over to enter the land the Lord your God is giving you, a land...promised you" (Deuteronomy 27:3). He told them to step out in faith before they received what was being given to them. They needed to take action in order to proceed into their promise.

There are seasons when no matter what we do, we will not be able to push the process along any quicker than it's intended to be. But there are other seasons when the breakthrough comes by way of us stirring up our courage and doing the thing we long to see in our lives before we behold it with our eyes. That's faith, and faith requires our action.

As you seek to access breakthrough and discern your next move, remember this: promises are full of grace, but they are not void of

APPENDIX

work. They are gifts and they are rewards. If you believe the words over your life to be true, however impossible they appear to be today, then it may be time for you to advance before you see fulfillment manifest.

Because at times the best choice you can make in your waiting is to get up and live today as though you already have received what you are longing to be given.

❧

THE CHOICE NOT TO DO

Back when I was about seven I had this strange tick. I can't remember how or why it began, but I started convincing myself that I needed to "reset" my knee every few steps. I would be walking somewhere and feel this impulse to bend my knee in order to do the necessary readjustment. It felt like my knee was locked up and this movement seemed to unstick whatever was so bothersome to me. Honestly, I don't even know what to say. It just was.

Later that year I went to the doctor's office for my annual checkup and, in true seven-year-old imaginative fashion, I was convinced I would be sent in for knee surgery. I braced myself for the worst answer to my problem as I walked into that patient room.

After all the typical pokes and prods, my sweet-natured doctor asked me if there was anything else I wanted to talk about. "Well, I have this knee problem," I explained. "Every few steps I have to reset my knee or it feels all weird and wrong." I went on to explain that this wasn't a choice I was making; I was being forced, even begged, to do exactly as I was doing to manage the problem.

When I was done, she softly smiled, looked right in my eyes, and said, "But what if you didn't?"

This is undoubtedly one of the most profound lessons I carry from my childhood. Because I took the advice to try and stop and, in utter amazement, it actually worked. I ceased doing the resetting and when I did, the tick went away never to compel me again. It was pure, tangible freedom for a child.

When we talk about our choices while navigating the in-between seasons of life, the reality is that we all have our ticks. They're the places we feel urged to respond a certain way, especially when we wait and are convinced we can do nothing about it. We easily give into these responses when another thing doesn't go as planned, an offensive comment is spoken to us, or a victory happens for another person rather than for us.

Those defaults of ours can become so irresistible to us that we feel as though our only option is to acquiesce one more time. We become so pulled by that response in our lives that we eliminate our freedom of choice. We believe ourselves the victim. There we give in, over and over...and over again.

Those words that day, spoken to a seven-year-old, are still stuck in my head as I consider what my choices are in the middle of my waiting, tension, and unknown. Because every time I feel drawn to surrender into fear or self-condemnation, the question I hear is this: "But what if you didn't?"

What if you didn't retreat to that rejected or insecure cave? What if you didn't perceive that text or photo as a message that you're not wanted or loved? What if another day without breakthrough didn't send you into a tailspin confirming you'll never have, always want, and forever be without? What if you stop yourself before you go down that ugly road of comparison? What if you simply didn't?

While some responses are quickly dealt with by this shift of mindset and intention, I'm also aware that others don't fall as easily into this category. Given how long you've done them or how deeply they are ingrained in your normal routine, they may require support through professional or pastoral counseling. Because when it comes to specific defaults or habits, you need a team to walk with you toward freedom. So this simple revelation of a seven-year-old is not a one-time fix for all troubles.

Yet for certain responses, these words are a straightforward key that offer you the opportunity of choice. When you feel as though you are without power and control in your waiting, there are areas where you can decide to respond differently. Your actions aren't determined by the circumstances around you, the season you're in, or the people who are seemingly surpassing you. They are yours and you have the opportunity to change them at any time.

Sometimes the shift comes from simply deciding not to do the thing that keeps leading you into the same despair, worry, insecurity, or self-condemnation. Each time you don't give in, you gain your voice back over your decisions and responses to your season. You actually move yourself into greater empowerment. Before anything externally shifts, you start living the life you dream of by resolving that you're not submitting yourself one day longer to the old pattern.

When you change your habits and stop making those same unhealthy choices, you take back control of your responses. You submit your decisions not to your feelings in the moment or what has happened in the past but to what God is saying and promising ahead.

Sometimes as you wait, one of the best choices you can make is to simply stop doing the thing you usually do and try something new. To exchange your response that pulls you down for one that lifts you up. No external circumstance or voice can make that choice for you. It's the small act of responding a different way, one decision at a time.

⁂

THE CHOICE TO GET BACK UP

I met my best friend Erin in college when we were "set-up" by a mutual friend of ours. I had just transferred to a small liberal arts college in North Carolina and was desperately looking to make friends. A guy I knew had recently graduated from the same school and was convinced Erin and I would hit it off, so he made the connection. Thankfully, Erin took his recommendation as an indication I was way cooler than I actually was and we hung out. All it took was one long lunch date over Thai food and the friendship was sealed. I can't imagine my college season without her, all thanks to that simple introduction. More than a decade later, we still set aside time for phone dates and family visits.

What I love most about our calls is that they aren't centered on what has happened since the last time we talked. We definitely share the important details, but mostly we process through what we're learning. Both Erin and I are deep thinkers so I love getting to hear what's stirring in her mind. Plus, she's a keen listener with an ability to add insight into whatever I share.

On a phone call a couple years ago, I was tuned in like usual to catch whatever treasures Erin might pass on to me as we talked through what was percolating in our minds. She launched into this story about a recent conversation she had in which the woman told Erin she was in the advanced level at her dance studio. Erin found herself somewhat surprised by this since the woman didn't appear to be as young or agile as one might imagine a high-caliber dancer to be.

Inquiring on how they determine such placements, this woman shared that she's not in that class because of her precise execution of skills or unprecedented fluidity. Rather, she's in it for one specific ability: her quick recovery. At her studio the teacher groups those who can get up the quickest when they fall to perform together. The requirement of perfection matters little. Expertise is about quick recovery.

I've never forgotten those words. They resonate with someone like me. I'm constantly tripping up and then wondering when I'll start moving ahead more easily, quickly, and seamlessly. But the truth is, we will slip up no matter how many times we determine we won't respond with that tick or swirl in those fears. There will come a time when it will happen.

When I was standing on that Irish cliff I realized even deeper my need to press into what God was doing in the now and not spin from all the recurring lies. But that encounter didn't make it so I never was overwhelmed with feelings of inadequacy, imperfection, or comparison. They still returned.

But when we recognize that we have a choice in how we respond and what we do, then when we mess up we can decide that we don't have to stay there. Maturity in the waiting looks a lot like choosing to recover quickly when we trip over some familiar obstacle one more time. It means learning to pick up our feet a little higher and be more aware of those entanglements. And it means swiftly getting back up and going again, shaking off what happened and continuing to carry vision for where God is leading us.

Here are some of the best questions you can ask when you fail to do what you wish you had done: How quickly can I recover? How fast can I get myself back up and in truth? How swiftly can I return to living my story, showing up to my day, and engaging in what God is up to?

Choice in the waiting and for the breakthrough often looks like arising and standing tall. It means dusting off your shoulders of the old familiar junk and refocusing your eyes on where God is leading and where you are going.

❦

THE CHOICE TO TAKE BACK

When I feel most overwhelmed by the demands of my day I can begin to believe that if I just survive today, then tomorrow I will thrive. It's probably my optimism that keeps me believing for tomorrow's green grass of goodness.

I think there's a lot to benefit from that mentality. I keep looking ahead with hope, motivating me to push forward past obstacles. But I also can inadvertently negate today's possibilities in expectation for what comes next. I can be so quick to decide that since today doesn't have room for things, tomorrow will carry my hope.

This looks a lot like waiting for tomorrow instead of living in today. We set tomorrow as the day we will rest, get healthy, risk, or accomplish. And we withhold our presence from today where we actually find ourselves. When this happens, we end up neglecting our present day due to this false idea that tomorrow will grant us the space to expel life's anxious air, fulfill dreams, and inhale fresh inspiration. Tomorrow becomes a picture of anticipated breakthrough while today remains only about survival.

One day I found myself so exhausted by my perpetual pattern

that I ended up asking myself whether I have painted tomorrow's fate by deciding today does not have time for my dreams, rest, or wonder. Am I suffocating life from today by only hoping for tomorrow? That's when I realized that it was time to take back today's promises.

It's easy to complain about waiting for God in certain areas of our lives. Yet all the while we can withhold from ourselves what does not have to be waited upon. In fact, I wonder if maybe waiting wouldn't feel as endless if we didn't pile on it all that is actually for us today.

I mean things like rest. It's easy to narrow it down to a concept of time and space, planning for that day far off when you will finally take a moment to exhale and renew your weary spirit. Or levels of fulfillment that are right before your eyes. You may not be married, but are you investing in your current relationships and community? You may not be in ministry as you dream of being one day, but what about your neighbor or the high school students down the street? Have you taken notice of the opportunities around you to serve and love?

You may even feel endlessly stuck in whatever this day holds and yet the question for you is, Are you aware of what is actually taking place in your life today?

When you are wrapped up in what's ahead, you easily miss the present. You can take what is for today and turn it into a rarely-experienced wish for some time in the future. Yet God longs to deposit what is accessible into your midst. You can reap dreams, health, or rest today if you stop putting them off as stock on the shelves for tomorrow.

One of the best choices you can make in your waiting is to take back those promises by showing up and living this day. To recognize what you have with a grateful heart and steward what is before you well, faithfully, and with intention.

How much fuller, freer, and more joyful would life be in an instant if you stopped believing tomorrow holds all fulfillment? What if, instead, you reclaim the joys of tomorrow as the gifts of today?

৯৮

THE CHOICE TO REST IN

There's one final response we can choose in the middle of the waiting and that is to rest deeply into today with all that it is and all that it is not.

Richard Rohr is a powerful voice of contemplation and spirituality. He often has me stirring as I read through his writings. In one section of his book, *Everything Belongs*, he talks about how to live fully and intentionally in the current moment, something I struggle to foster especially when waiting.

As I mentioned in the previous section, we're fairly prone to anticipate and dream for what is next. Yet we often fail to realize that in our striving to grasp what's ahead, we can inadvertently proclaim that what is present today is not enough. Channeling all our attention, energy, and strength to the future reveals that we lack gratitude for what the current moment holds. We can unintentionally develop an entire rhythm in our lives where we only look forward to what will be and miss exactly what is. We remain unsatisfied by all that makes up the moment right now. We miss life.

There's irony intricately woven into this approach. In an attempt to receive whatever it is we desperately wait for, we miss out on all that actually is. We miss the good and the hard and even the breakthroughs, because we have trained ourselves to seek and plan for what's next.

Our present is pushed to the outer realms of our focus by our striving to receive what we will never consciously live in because we are only ever looking ahead.

It's a cycle of monumental cost.

But there's a different way to approach our waiting and forthcoming breakthroughs, one that channels our attention and perception to our lives and has us participate in the middle of what is alive and breathing. And that is recognizing that whatever it is, "it's okay as it is. This moment is as perfect as it can be. The saints called it the 'sacrament of the present moment.'"[1]

Whatever it is, it's okay as it is.

I have found such freedom in these simple words that allow me to exhale amid the pressure I feel to move myself forward. My waiting, with all its mess and emotions and rawness, is okay as it is. My longing for something more is okay as it is. But also my current moment of desire and tension is okay as it is. There is no need to fast-track my way out of it. No rush to fix it. Rather, the choice available to me is to be present right in it. I am able to feel my pain, anger, and tiredness as it comes—and to recognize the joy, gifts, and grace of what is.

Because as Rohr powerfully captures it, "God is either in this now or God isn't at all."[2] And believing that God is, in fact, in this moment means that I want to be in this now with him. Otherwise I miss out on the beautiful gift of partnership and relationship that is extended my way to help me navigate today. What I mean is that I will miss doing life with God if I am too focused on receiving whatever comes next.

---

1. Richard Rohr, *Everything Belongs* (Chestnut Ridge, NY: Crossroad Publishing Company, 1999). 54.

2. Ibid.

When I am anxious about my current reality, antsy for movement and feeling pressure for breakthrough, it is time for me to stop, breathe, and allow those simple words to wash over me once again.

Whatever is, is okay.

This is my reality and God is with me in it. Though it's hard, unexpected, or long, it's still okay because Emmanuel is here. And where he is, is where I want to be as well. It's where I belong, thrive, and become.

As I do this more intentionally in my life, I find those pressures that the world places on me to get moving, advancing, and pushing to fall away. I remember again the choice I am empowered to make. To look at my now and say, "You are my gift that I recognize and accept for all that you are and all that you aren't. You are okay as you are." I lean into this day, not missing out on it by the false belief that somehow ahead, if I ever arrive there, I will start living there.

Because the choices you make today in the middle of your waiting have everything to do with your presence in the breakthroughs you believe for ahead. But first you must decide that today is okay as it is, for that is the gateway to participate in what comes next.

God with you here. God with you now.

ABOUT THE AUTHOR

Caroline Schandel is a passionate communicator with a desire to awaken this generation to experience God's fullness. Throughout her twenties she travelled around the world and came alive as she witnessed God moving in powerful ways. Today she encourages and inspires others to meet God in the middle of their stories and seasons. She completed her Masters of Divinity from Gordon-Conwell Theological Seminary and resides in Atlanta with her husband, Mark, and their growing family.

Connect more with her at CarolineSchandel.com.